Historic Walks
in and around
Newcastle

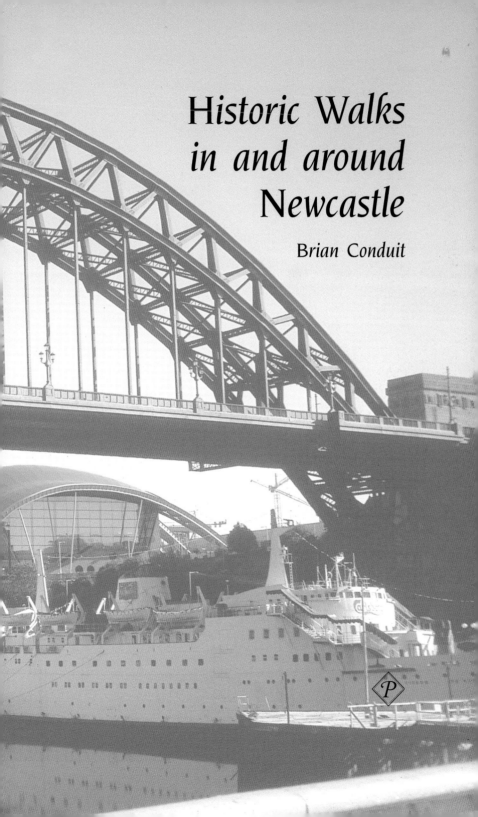

Historic Walks
in and around
Newcastle

Brian Conduit

First published in 2008
by Palatine Books,
Carnegie House,
Chatsworth Road
Lancaster LA1 4SL
www.palatinebooks.com

British Library Cataloguing-in-Publication data
A catalogue record for this book is available from the British Library

ISBN: 978-1-874181-52-1

Designed and typeset by Carnegie Book Production
www.carnegiebookproduction.com
Printed and bound in the UK by Alden Press

Contents

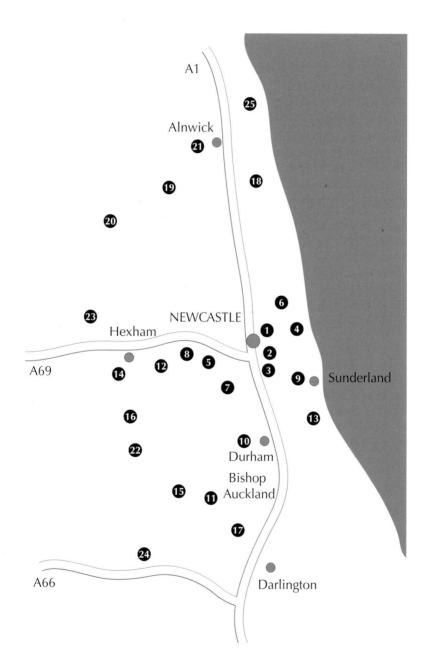

A1

Alnwick

NEWCASTLE

Hexham

A69

Sunderland

Durham

Bishop
Auckland

A66

Darlington

Introduction to Newcastle and the surrounding area

Both its location and its architecture make Newcastle-upon-Tyne one of the most visually exciting cities in Britain. It is situated above the steep northern banks of the river which is crossed by an astonishing number and variety of road, rail and foot bridges. It is one of the few large cities to possess a medieval castle. In the early nineteenth century the centre was redeveloped by two architects, Grainger and Dobson, and their handsome and dignified classical buildings have bestowed on Newcastle one of the finest city centres in the country. In more recent years some stunning examples of modern architecture have appeared both in Newcastle itself and across the bridges on the revitalised Gateshead side of the river.

Newcastle has a longer history than most of Britain's other great provincial cities. It began its life as early as the second century AD as a fort on Hadrian's Wall, named Pons Aelius. Around 900 years later the eldest son of William the Conqueror founded a castle above the Tyne – the 'New Castle' which gave the city its name. Throughout the Middle Ages it was in the front line of the many wars with Scotland and was defended by a line of walls as well as the castle. From the sixteenth century onwards the coal trade along the Tyne developed and by the eighteenth century Newcastle had become an important coal exporting port. During the industrial heyday of the Victorian era, it became a major centre for shipbuilding and heavy engineering but following the decline of its traditional industries in the twentieth century, it has transformed itself and is seeking a new role as a cultural centre and provider of service industries.

Surrounding the city is an area steeped in history which boasts two World Heritage Sites. One of these is Hadrian's Wall, the grandest Roman monument in Britain and one of the finest in Europe. The other is the magnificent medieval complex of cathedral and castle towering above the River Wear at Durham.

As a result of the proximity of the Scottish border and the many wars with Scotland, there is a greater concentration of castles here than anywhere else in the country. Some of these – Alnwick and Warkworth – rank among the finest in England. Stately homes are scattered throughout the area, ranging from modest manor houses to great Georgian and Victorian mansions.

Coal was mined around Newcastle from early times and the area became one of the major centres of the Industrial Revolution. It was this part of the country that pioneered the development of the railways. Wooden horse-drawn wagonways were built to make it easier to transport coal from the pits to the nearest rivers. In the early nineteenth century wooden rails and horses were replaced by iron rails and steam-hauled locomotives. Some of the old wagonways and former railway tracks that once served the collieries have been converted into footpaths and cycleways and the world's oldest railway bridge, the Causey Arch, survives as a striking monument to the beginnings of the railways. Relics of an older industry – lead mining – can also be found in parts of the region.

Newcastle also has the advantage of lying at the heart of some of the most attractive and varied countryside in England. For a start there is a superb coastline, not only in rural Northumberland but also in previously coal scarred Durham where the National Trust and local authorities have done a magnificent job in restoring this coast to something like its previous tranquillity and attractiveness. The pleasant walking in the valleys of the main rivers – Tyne, Wear, Tees and Coquet – is augmented by a series of interesting old towns and villages, such as Barnard Castle, Stanhope, Hexham, Corbridge, Alnwick, Rothbury and Warkworth. Excellent walking is to be had in the hill country – the dales of the North Pennines and on the Simonside and Cheviot Hills.

Two National Trails traverse the region. The Pennine Way runs north-south on its way from Derbyshire to the Scottish Borders and for several miles coincides with the east-west Hadrian's Wall Path. Where the two trails run together is one of the most memorable and atmospheric spots in the whole region, looking across a wide and largely empty landscape from the South Tyne valley to the edge of the Border Forest and along the finest surviving stretch of Hadrian's Wall, a magnificent combination of scenery and history.

Useful addresses

The Ramblers' Association, 2nd Floor, Camelford House, 87–90 Albert Embankment, London SE1 7TW Tel: 020 7339 8500

The National Trust, PO Box 39, Warrington WA5 7WD Tel: 0870 458 4000

English Heritage, Customer Services Department, PO Box 569, Swindon SN2 2YP Tel: 0870 333 1181

Local Tourist Information Centres:

Alnwick 01665 510665
Barnard Castle 01833 690909/695320
Beamish 0191 370 2533
Bishop Auckland 01388 602610
Corbridge 01434 220616
Craster 01665 576007
Durham 0191 384 3720
Hexham 01434 652220
Morpeth 01670 500700
Newcastle-upon-Tyne 0191 277 8000/478 4222
North Shields 0191 200 5895
Otterburn 01830 520093
Rothbury 01669 620887
South Shields 0191 454 6612
Sunderland 0191 553 2000
Whitley Bay 0191 200 8535

Public transport

For information about bus and train services either phone Traveline on 0870 608 2608 or contact the local tourist information centre

The Walks

The sketch maps are only a rough guide and you should always take with you an Ordnance Survey (O.S.) map. The best maps for walkers are the Explorer maps and the number and title of the relevant ones are given in the introductory information for each route.

Visiting historic sites

Some of the historic buildings and sites featured in the walks are open all the year round and are free to look round but most have restricted opening times and charge an entrance fee. In particular some English Heritage properties and most stately homes are closed during the winter months, approximately from the end of October to around Easter time. In order to avoid disappointment, it is always best to enquire about opening times by contacting either the individual site or the nearest tourist information centre. The relevant phone numbers are provided.

Walk map key

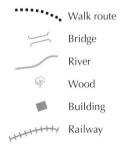

Walk route

Bridge

River

Wood

Building

Railway

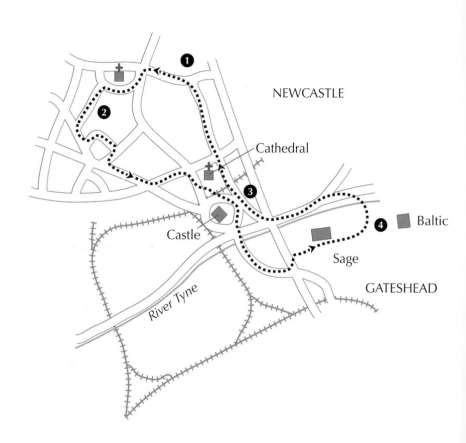

NEWCASTLE

Cathedral

Baltic

Castle

Sage

GATESHEAD

River Tyne

HISTORIC WALKS IN AND AROUND NEWCASTLE

WALK 1

Newcastle and Gateshead

LENGTH:	4.8 km (3 miles)
TIME:	1.5 hours
TERRAIN:	Easy town walking, some steps
START/PARKING:	Newcastle upon Tyne, Grey's Monument at the top of Grey Street, GR NZ248645. Car parks in Newcastle city centre
BUS/TRAIN:	Newcastle is easily reached by train and bus from all the local towns
REFRESHMENTS:	Plenty of pubs, cafes and restaurants in Newcastle and Gateshead
MAP:	O.S. Explorer 316 – Newcastle upon Tyne or pick up a town map from the Tourist Information Centre

Between Newcastle and Gateshead the River Tyne, crossed by a multitude and variety of bridges, flows through a virtual gorge and the steep banks on both sides help to create one of the most dramatic and exciting city skylines in the country. Nowadays Newcastle and Gateshead are bracketed together and marketed as one for the purposes of tourism. This walk embraces all the major historic monuments of Newcastle plus the new developments and refurbished quaysides on both sides of the river.

ⓘ Grey's Monument is the major landmark in the centre of
Newcastle. It was erected in 1838 to commemorate Earl
Grey, a member of an aristocratic Northumbrian family
and the Prime Minister responsible for passing the Great
Reform Act of 1832. By substantially increasing the number
of people eligible to vote, this act paved the way for full
Parliamentary democracy.

The monument, 41m (135 feet) high, stands at the top
of the sloping, curving Grey Street, lined by dignified
buildings and widely acclaimed as one of the finest
streets in the country. It was constructed as part of the
redevelopment of Newcastle by two architects Dobson
and Grainger in the 1830s. With its wide streets and fine
architecture, the whole area, called Grainger Town, gives

A stretch of Newcastle's medieval wall

The twelfth-century keep of the 'New Castle' above the Tyne

Newcastle arguably the finest city centre in the country. The length of Grey Street is walked at the end of this route, a fitting finale.

❶ Begin by facing down Grey Street and turn right along Blackett Street, between Eldon Square Shopping Centre on the left and – a little further on – Old Eldon Square on the right. Pass under an arch, turn left into Newgate Street and turn right along St Andrews Street, passing to the left of St Andrew's church.

ⓘ St Andrew's is the oldest church in Newcastle and dates back to the twelfth century. Since then it has been enlarged on several occasions but retains some of its original Norman architecture, especially the outstanding chancel arch.

🚶 **Keep ahead towards the arch leading into Chinatown and the stands of Newcastle United football ground and just beyond the arch, turn left onto a path that keeps by one of the best surviving stretches of Newcastle's medieval walls.**

ⓘ In the Middle Ages the walls of Newcastle were around 3.2 km (2 miles) in circumference but now this stretch by Stowell Street and the adjoining stretch in Bath Lane is all that is left, apart from another sizeable chunk behind Central Station. The walls were begun in the thirteenth century, mainly as a protection against Scottish raids, and regularly upgraded

🚶 **Just before reaching a corner tower, turn left through an arch in the wall, cross Stowell Street (lined with Chinese restaurants) and keep ahead along Friar Street to Blackfriars. ❷**

ⓘ Blackfriars is an oasis of calm amidst the noise and bustle of the city centre. This is appropriate as it was originally a Dominican friary founded in the thirteenth century. Many of the domestic buildings survived the destruction of the church at the Reformation but after being put to a variety of purposes, they had become derelict by the middle of the twentieth century and were within a whisker of being pulled down. Following successful restoration in the 1980s they are now used as craft workshops and one is a restaurant.

ⓧ Return to Stowell Street, turn left and left again beside
another stretch of the medieval wall on Bath Lane.
Turn left into Cross Street, walk along the east side
of Charlotte Square and turn right into Fenkle Street.
Continue along it, passing the eighteenth-century
Assembly Rooms, to Westgate Road and bear left.

Cross Grainger Street by the church of St John the
Baptist and at a road junction bear slightly left to
continue along Collingwood Street. At the next junction,
turn right to pass in front of the cathedral. A little further
on, turn left under the Black Gate, cross a footbridge
over some of the foundations of the castle, go under a
railway bridge and ahead is the impressive Norman keep
of the castle. ❸

ⓘ Newcastle's mainly fourteenth-century cathedral is the
former parish church of St Nicholas, raised to cathedral
status in 1882. It is particularly noted for its striking crown
spire, added in the late fifteenth century, a feature usually
only found north of the border.

The Norman 'new castle' that gives the city its name
was founded in 1080 by Robert, eldest son of William the
Conqueror. Its twelfth-century keep is one of the finest in
England. The thirteenth-century Black Gate, surmounted
by a later building, was the castle gatehouse but became
separated from the keep by the building of the railway
across the castle precincts in the nineteenth century. Tel:
0191 232 7938

ⓧ Walk beside the keep and descend a long flight of steps,
initially by more castle remains, to the Quayside. Cross
a road at the bottom and keep ahead to cross the Swing
Bridge over the River Tyne into Gateshead.

The stunning new Sage building at Gateshead lies between the Tyne and Millennium Bridges

ⓘ The River Tyne is crossed by an astonishing variety of bridges – road, rail and pedestrian – dating from the nineteenth, twentieth and twenty-first centuries. The four closest and most striking ones begin chronologically with the High Level Bridge, built in 1849 by Robert Stephenson. This remarkable two-tiered structure, a triumph of Victorian engineering, carries both road and railway across the river. Next comes the Swing Bridge, built in 1876 and designed by William Armstrong. The majestic Tyne Bridge, opened in 1929, was built by the same company that was responsible for Sydney Harbour Bridge. Lastly is the graceful and spectacular Millennium Bridge, a unique tilting pedestrian bridge that opened in 2001.

ⓧ The road curves slightly left uphill, passing in front of the Hilton Hotel. Take the first road on the left to pass under the Tyne Bridge and bear right up a sloping path to the Sage. To the right is St Mary's church, now the Gateshead Visitor Centre.

The Tyne Bridge soars majestically across the river, dwarfing the Norman castle

Walk through the Sage and out the other side into Performance Square. Descend steps, walk through a car park towards the Baltic Centre for Contemporary Art and descend more steps to the river opposite the Millennium Bridge. ❹

ℹ The collection of new buildings and renovation of old ones on the Gateshead side of the river marks a change of fortune in a town that had been declining for years with the collapse of its industries and which had always been

View from the Millennium Bridge, most recent of the many bridges over the Tyne between Newcastle and Gateshead

regarded as the poor relation of its bigger neighbour on the other side of the river. The Visitor Centre, housed in a former church, is a good starting point to find out more of the history of Gateshead. The Sage, a concert hall and music centre, is a truly stunning modern building, designed by Sir Norman Foster and opened in 2004. The Baltic Centre for Contemporary Art is housed in a redundant flour mill, a handsome building in its own right.

ⓧ **Cross the Millennium Bridge – a memorable experience – back into Newcastle and turn left along the Quayside. Pass under the Tyne Bridge again and follow the road as it swings right away from the river. ❺ To the left is the Guildhall and opposite it is Besse Surtees' House.**

❶ Besse Surtees' House is actually two adjacent merchant's houses of the sixteenth and seventeenth centuries. They are a particularly fine example of the domestic architecture of the period. Tel: 0191 261 1585

ⓧ **The road curves left uphill and goes under a railway bridge. Bear right to continue up Dean Street and at a crossroads, keep ahead up Grey Street to return to the start.**

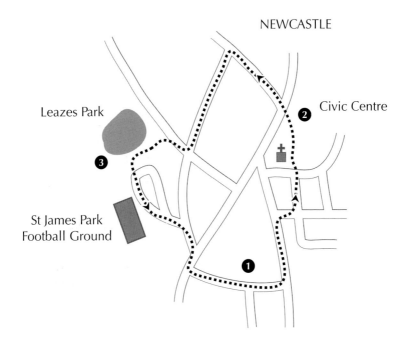

NEWCASTLE

Leazes Park

Civic Centre

2

St James Park
Football Ground

3

1

WALK 2

Newcastle: Civic Centre and Leazes Park

LENGTH:	3.2 km (2 miles)
TIME:	1 hour
TERRAIN:	Flat and easy town walking
START/PARKING:	Newcastle upon Tyne, Grey's Monument at top of Grey Street, GR NZ248645. Car parks in Newcastle city centre
BUS/TRAIN:	Newcastle is easily reached by train and bus from all the local towns
REFRESHMENTS:	Plenty of pubs, cafes and restaurants in Newcastle
MAP:	O.S. Explorer 316 – Newcastle upon Tyne or pick up a town map from the Tourist Information Centre

This second walk in Newcastle city centre concentrates on the modern Civic Centre, the University Quarter and the elegant nineteenth-century architecture of Leazes Terrace. It also includes a brief excursion into the beautiful greenery of Leazes Park, recently restored to its Victorian splendour.

❶ With your back to the Eldon Square Shopping Centre, walk along Blackett Street and turn first left into the pedestrianised Northumberland Street, one of Newcastle's main shopping thoroughfares. Turn right along Northumberland Road and take the first road on the left to the Civic Centre buildings.

The striking buildings of the Civic Centre, the seat of local government, were built in the 1960s. The opening ceremony in 1968 was performed by King Haakon of Norway, an event which emphasised the strong traditional links between Tyneside and the Scandinavian countries.

On the other side of the gardens is the church of St Thomas the Martyr. It was designed by John Dobson and built in 1830.

Walk across the gardens in front of the Civic Centre, bearing left to emerge onto a road (Barras Bridge). ❷ Cross the road at traffic lights and keep ahead – there is a statue of the famous Newcastle engineer Sir William Armstrong here – along Claremont Road, passing between university buildings.

The University of Newcastle upon Tyne began its life as a college of Durham University in 1851. Its rapid growth after the Second World War led to it becoming a separate institution in 1963.

At a crossroads turn left along Queen Victoria Road, between the university on the left and the Royal Victoria Infirmary on the right, and at a junction turn right into Richardson Road alongside Leazes Park on the left. Turn left into the park and keep ahead to a footpath sign where you bear right and head up steps to the lake, a beautiful spot. ❸

Newcastle Civic Centre

Leazes Park

ⓘ One of the great attractions of Leazes Park is its proximity to Newcastle city centre. It is the oldest park in the city, opened in 1873, and the lake is its focal point. The park has recently been attractively restored to something approaching its original design.

⊛ **In such surroundings you may well be tempted to stay longer and explore the park more thoroughly – perhaps doing a circuit of the lake – but the route continues to the left. After a few yards, turn left again away from the lake and keep ahead at a junction of paths to exit the park. Walk along the road ahead between Newcastle United's football ground (St James Park) on the right and Leazes Terrace on the left. Turn left into St James Terrace and look along the road on the left for a further view of Leazes Terrace.**

🛈 Richard Grainger, the man responsible for so much of the fine architecture in Newcastle city centre, built the two rows of dignified houses that make up Leazes Terrace around 1830. They retain much of the elegance of the earlier Georgian and Regency styles. Nowadays most of the houses are owned by Newcastle University.

🚶 **At a junction, take the first road on the right (Leazes Park Road), head down to a T-junction and turn right. Almost immediately turn left under an arch and walk along Blackett Street by the Eldon Square Shopping Centre to return to the start.**

The early nineteenth-century Leazes Terrace

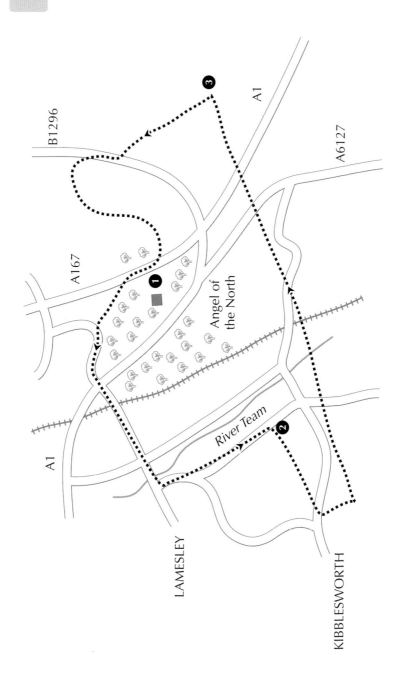

B1296

A1

A6127

A167

Angel of
the North

River Team

A1

LAMESLEY

KIBBLESWORTH

WALK 3

Angel of the North

LENGTH:	9.7 km (6 miles)
TIME:	3 hours
TERRAIN:	Field paths and a disused railway track, some walking along roads and lanes
START/PARKING:	Laybys beside the A167 just to the north of its junction with the A1 provide parking for visitors to the Angel of the North, GR NZ264580
BUS/TRAIN:	Buses from Newcastle and Gateshead
REFRESHMENTS:	Pub at Lamesley, pub at Kibblesworth
MAP:	O.S. Explorer 308 – Durham & Sunderland

The Angel of the North is the latest in a long line of imposing structures erected in the Newcastle area that includes Hadrian's Wall, Durham Cathedral, great medieval castles, country houses and a range of industrial and transport monuments. It dominates the surrounding area and can be seen throughout most of the route. Despite being on the fringe of urban Tyneside and bisected by the busy A1, parts of the walk have a surprisingly peaceful and rural feel.

❶ The Angel of the North, impressive enough when seen from a distance, is overwhelming close up. The statistics alone are staggering. It is Britain's largest sculpture, 20m (65 feet) high, 200 tonnes of weathering steel were used

The Angel of the North

in its construction and its wing span of 54m (175 feet) is almost that of a jumbo jet. Antony Gormley was chosen to be the sculptor and although his design inevitably met with opposition and controversy at first, the Angel has subsequently won many awards and become generally accepted. Its construction in 1997–98 took about 7 months.

① After a close look at the Angel, walk northwards along a tarmac path parallel to the A167 and at the end of a grassy area the path curves right onto the road. Continue along it and at a public footpath sign to Longacre Wood, turn left onto a tarmac path. Almost immediately bear

right downhill along a stony path to a footpath sign
where you bear left onto a path (a former railway line).
   Head downhill along this enclosed path to a road
and turn left. Continue downhill, curving left to cross a
bridge over the A1, and keep ahead over a railway bridge
to reach a crossroads by Lamesley church.

ⓘ The medieval church at Lamesley was rebuilt in 1759 and
restored in the nineteenth century. It overlooks Lamesley
Pastures, a rare – and almost miraculous – surviving
example in this built-up area of a largely unaltered
medieval landscape. Just to the south of the bridge over
the River Team, archaeologists have discovered the site of a
medieval village. The walk goes along the western edge of
the meadows.

The Angel of the North has now become a tourist attraction in its own right

⊛ Keep ahead, cross Lamesley Bridge over the little River Team and immediately turn left along a road signposted to Kibblesworth. At a junction keep ahead – take care as there is not much of a verge at times. – and after 800m (0.5 miles), turn right through a hedge gap, ❷ at a public footpath sign, and walk along the left edge of a field to a road. Turn right and at a public footpath sign on the edge of Kibblesworth, turn left through a kissing gate. For the pub keep ahead a few yards into the village.

After going through the kissing gate, walk first along the right edge of a field, then along an enclosed path and pass beside a barrier onto a track. Turn left along this straight track – a former railway line – and the buildings of Tyneside can be seen across the fields on the left. Cross a road, keep ahead between the lakes of Lamesley Reedbeds and continue over the River Team, under railway bridges and under three road bridges. The last of the road bridges is the A1 and the track now gently ascends to a crossways by a barn. Turn left through a gate, ❸ pass between farm buildings and continue along a track which emerges onto a road opposite the entrance to Ravensworth Golf Club. Cross over, turn right into Eighton Banks and at a public footpath sign, turn left along Black Lane.

Where the lane ends, keep ahead along a tree-lined track and just before reaching a road, turn left. Pass beside a barrier and continue along an enclosed path which heads gently downhill and bends right. At the end of the grassy area, turn left, passing under the A167, and at a footpath sign to Angel of the North, turn sharp left to return to the start.

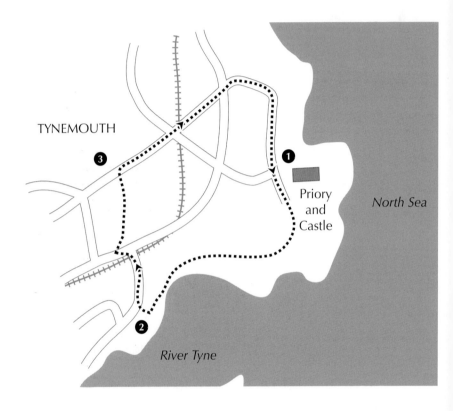

TYNEMOUTH

Priory
and
Castle

North Sea

River Tyne

THE GIBRALTER ROCK

BEACH CAFE

WALK 4

Tynemouth Castle and Priory

LENGTH:	4.8 km (3 miles)
TIME:	1.5 hours
TERRAIN:	Easy urban walking on tarmac paths by the river, through a park and along the coast
START/PARKING:	Tynemouth, at the end of Front Street in front of the castle and priory, GR NZ372695. Pay car parks at Tynemouth
BUS/TRAIN:	Buses and metro from Newcastle
REFRESHMENTS:	Pubs and cafes at Tynemouth
MAP:	O.S. Explorer 316 – Newcastle upon Tyne

Tynemouth village is based around the bold headland lying between the North Sea and the mouth of the River Tyne which is occupied by the dramatic ruins of a medieval castle and priory. This short walk, which starts by the headland, falls into three sections: the first part is along the river, with fine views across to South Shields on the opposite bank, then comes a stretch along roads and through a park, and the finale is along the promenade above Tynemouth's fine sandy beaches.

ℹ The headland at Tynemouth is unusual in having a military and religious building on the same site, as the priory is enclosed by the walls of the castle. The religious settlement came first as the original monastery was founded here in the seventh century. This was destroyed during the Viking raids of the ninth century but was refounded by the Normans in the late eleventh century as a Benedictine priory. Its remains are extensive and include the lower part of the elaborate west front, the impressive thirteenth-century east end, still standing to its full height, and a small but well preserved fifteenth-century chapel.

The powerful castle walls were built towards the end of the thirteenth century, chiefly to protect this highly strategic location from Scottish raids, and they enclosed one of the

Gatehouse and barbican at Tynemouth Castle

Castle and priory overlooking the beach at Tynemouth

largest fortified areas in the country. The gatehouse, with its barbican or outer defence, was added in the fourteenth century and the castle was further strengthened in the fifteenth century. After Henry VIII dissolved the priory in 1539, the castle was retained as a royal fortress and has been updated and used as a gun battery in later conflicts, including the Napoleonic Wars and both the First and Second World Wars. Tel: 0191 257 1090

❶ **Start by facing the castle and priory and turn right down Pier Road. After crossing a bridge at the bottom, take the path ahead, signposted to Fish Quay and Collingwood Monument, and on emerging into an open grassy area, turn left up to the Collingwood Monument.**

Tynemouth Priory from the Castle

ⓘ This huge and imposing monument was erected in the 1840s to commemorate Admiral Lord Collingwood. Born in Newcastle in 1748, Collingwood joined the Royal Navy and rose quickly through the ranks along with another promising new recruit, Nelson. He saw action during the American War of Independence and during the Napoleonic Wars became one of Nelson's principal lieutenants. At the Battle of Trafalgar in 1805 he played a major role, taking command after Nelson's death. He died at sea in 1810 and was buried in St Paul's Cathedral.

At a footpath sign above the mouth of the River Tyne, turn right onto a tarmac path, at a fork take the left hand lower path and at the bottom, bear right along the concrete promenade by the river. Where the promenade ends just in front of the Fish Quay, ❷ turn right by the Low Lights car park to a road and turn right again, heading uphill along Tanners Bank. Go under a bridge to a T-junction, turn left and after about 91m (100 yards), turn right into Northumberland Park.

Follow a broad, winding tarmac track through the park, descending to pass to the left of a pool then heading uphill and bending right to emerge onto a road via a gate. ❸ Turn right to a roundabout and keep ahead, passing a long and imposing Edwardian terrace on the left (Percy Park) to reach the seafront. Turn right above the sandy beach to return to the start.

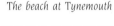

The beach at Tynemouth

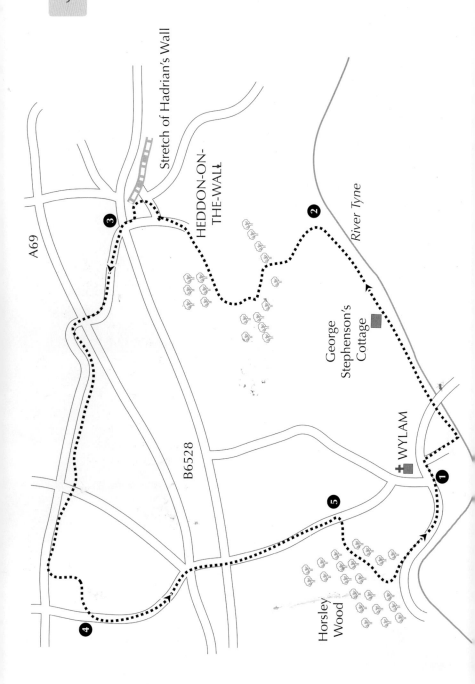

Stretch of Hadrian's Wall

HEDDON-ON-
THE-WALL

River Tyne

A69

George
Stephenson's
Cottage

B6528

WYLAM

Horsley
Wood

WALK 5

Tyne Valley between Wylam and Heddon-on-the-Wall

LENGTH:	13.7 km (8.5 miles)
TIME:	4 hours
TERRAIN:	Riverside, woodland and field paths and tracks; some road walking and one steady climb
START/PARKING:	Wylam, road junction in village centre just below the church, GR NZ114646. Roadside parking at Wylam
BUS/TRAIN:	Buses and trains from Newcastle and Hexham
REFRESHMENTS:	Pubs and café at Wylam, snacks and soft drinks at George Stephenson's Cottage, pubs and tea shop at Heddon-on-the-Wall
MAP:	O.S. Explorer 316 – Newcastle upon Tyne

A pleasant walk beside the River Tyne brings you to the cottage in which George Stephenson, one of the earliest and most prominent pioneers of railway development was born. You then head up to Heddon-on-the-Wall, where an impressive stretch of Hadrian's Wall can be seen, and this is followed by a walk along the line of the wall. Fine views reward you on the descent back into the Tyne valley and the finale is an attractive walk through sloping woodland with some dramatic, high-level views over the river.

(walking icon) **❶ Begin by walking along Main Road, signposted to Station and George Stephenson's Cottage, and take the first road on the right. At a public footpath sign to River Tyne, keep ahead along a track which bends first right and then left. Where it bends right again, keep ahead along a path through trees heading down to the river. This attractive path curves left through trees above the Tyne. Continue along a road in front of cottages and where it bends left, keep ahead down steps and along a path to pass under Wylam Bridge.**

Climb steps, walk along a road and at a National Trust sign for George Stephenson's Birthplace, go through a kissing gate and continue along an enclosed path above the river. After emerging from the trees, walk across a picnic area and at the far end, turn left and go through a kissing gate onto a track in front of George Stephenson's Cottage.

ⓘ The great rail engineer George Stephenson was born in 1781 and lived for the first eight years of his life in one room of this humble eighteenth-century cottage, now owned by the National Trust. Three other families lived in the rest of the house. Like his father he went to work in the local collieries. Despite no education, this self-taught man used his enquiring mind to advance his knowledge and quickly achieved promotion.

Like other colliery engineers at the time, he experimented with building a steam locomotive to pull the coal wagons currently hauled by horses between the mines and the rivers and in 1825 his Locomotion No 1 successfully pulled wagons on the Stockton to Darlington Railway. In 1830 came the opening of the first passenger railway in the world, the Liverpool to Manchester Railway, drawn by Stephenson's Rocket which had won a series of trials against its competitors during the previous year. This event marked the real beginning of the 'Railway Age' that was to revolutionise the country over the next 30 years.

George's son Robert followed in his father's footsteps and became an even greater rail engineer, particularly famous for his magnificent bridges and viaducts, including the High Level Bridge over the Tyne at Newcastle and the Royal Border Bridge across the Tweed at Berwick. George's work caused him to move to Derbyshire and his huge wealth enabled him to purchase a large country house near Chesterfield. He died there in 1848.

Bridge over the River Tyne at Wylam

The track beside the cottage was the Newcastle to Hexham road but in the eighteenth century it became a waggonway linking Wylam Colliery to the coal staithes further down the Tyne. Originally the coal wagons were pulled by horses on wooden rails but in the early nineteenth century iron rails replaced the wooden ones and steam locomotives, pioneered by George Stephenson and others, later replaced the horses. Tel: 01661 853457

ⓧ **Turn right along the disused railway track and after nearly 1.2 km (0.75 miles), turn left through a kissing gate, at a public footpath sign to Heddon-on-the-Wall, to join the Hadrian's Wall Path. ❷ Head straight across a golf course and on the far side continue along an uphill path through woodland. This is the start of a steady climb of nearly 2.4 km (1.5 miles). By some buildings turn right to continue uphill through woodland and on emerging from the trees, keep ahead along an enclosed track. The track turns right and becomes a lane which continues up into Heddon-on-the-Wall.**

❶ On this part of the walk there is a fine view to the right over the Tyne valley. The lower slopes were the site of the battle of Newburn Ford between the English and Scots in 1640. The Scottish army was camped on the north side of the river and the English on the south. The Scottish army won this encounter by bombarding the English with cannon mounted on the tower of Newburn church, later fording the Tyne – there was no bridge at that time – and scattering the English forces.

ⓧ **At a Hadrian's Wall Path sign turn right along Towne Gate, curving left to a footpath post.**

❶ A brief detour ahead brings you to a fine stretch of Hadrian's Wall, 200m (656 feet) long.

🚶 At the footpath post turn left along a track between houses, bear left in front of a wall and continue along an enclosed, tree-lined path to a road. Turn right to the main road, cross it to the Three Tuns pub and turn left beside the pub along the Military Road ❸

ℹ️ The Military Road was constructed by the Duke of Cumberland at the time of the Jacobite Rebellion in 1745 in order to make it easier to move his troops between the western and eastern ends of the Scottish border. Much of it was built on the foundations of Hadrian's Wall, one of the main reasons for the disappearance of most of this part of the wall.

🚶 For much of the next 3.2 km (2 miles) you are walking along the line of the Roman wall, although there is nothing to see of it. One deviation from the line is where the road bends right to cross the A69 and immediately turns left. At this point you climb a stile to walk along a path parallel to the road, much pleasanter than walking on the road itself. Where the road bears right to rejoin the line of the wall, turn left over a stile, descend steps and walk by the right edge of a field parallel to the road.

Continue along the right edge of several fields and the path eventually curves left to a gate. Go through onto a lane by Rudchester Farm and go through the gate opposite. The land around the farm occupies the site of the Roman fort of Vindobala. Keep ahead along a grassy path, turn right alongside a wire fence on the left and in the field corner, turn left over a stile. Keep along the right edge of the next two fields and in the corner of the second field, turn left – here leaving the line of the wall – to continue along the right field edge. Follow the path around a right bend to emerge onto a lane. ❹

Turn left, at a roundabout keep ahead to cross a bridge over the A69 and at a crossroads continue

George Stephenson's Cottage at Wylam

downhill towards Wylam. At this point you could keep
on the road to the start but a more attractive finale is
to turn right through a kissing gate at a public footpath
sign to Ovingham Road. ❺ This is just after passing a
Welcome to Wylam notice. Walk along the right edge
of a field and go through a kissing gate to enter Horsley
Wood.

Walk along a most attractive path that keeps along
the left inside edge of the steeply sloping woodland,
later curving left to give superb views over the river and
Wylam Bridge. Eventually you descend to go through a
kissing gate onto a road and turn left to return to the
start.

A short stretch of Hadrian's Wall at Heddon-on-the-Hill

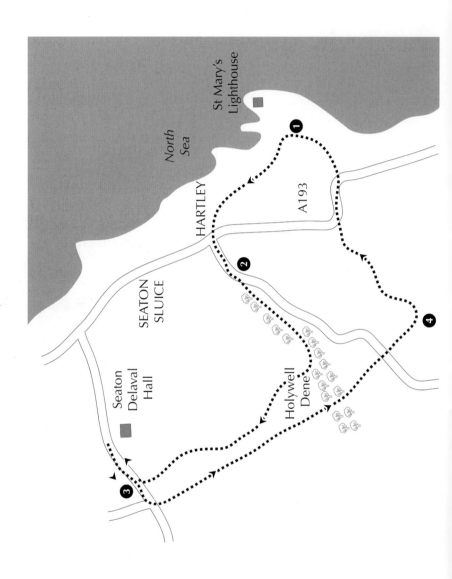

St Mary's
Lighthouse

*North
Sea*

HARTLEY

A193

SEATON
SLUICE

Seaton
Delaval
Hall

Holywell
Dene

THE DELAVAL ARMS.

WALK 6
NE26 4QR

Holywell Dene and Seaton Delaval Hall

Seaton Delaval Hall

LENGTH:	12.9 km (8 miles)
TIME:	4 hours
TERRAIN:	Mainly flat walking along a combination of easy to follow coast, woodland and field paths
START/PARKING:	St Mary's Island, signposted from the A193 to the north of Whitley Bay, GR NZ351750
BUS/TRAIN:	Buses from Newcastle
REFRESHMENTS:	Pub at Hartley, cafe at St Mary's Island, tea room at Seaton Delaval Hall during opening times
MAP:	Explorer 316 – Newcastle upon Tyne

Although a flat walk, there is plenty of variety. From the start the views extend along sandy beaches from Blyth in the north across to Whitley Bay and the mouth of the River Tyne to the south. After an opening short stretch along the coast to the north of the lighthouse on St Mary's Island, the walk continues through part of a beautiful wooded dene. From here you head across fields to Seaton Delaval Hall, an imposing eighteenth-century house. A disused railway track leads back to the dene and more field paths return you to the starting point.

St Mary's Lighthouse

ⓘ The small, rocky St Mary's Island is reached by a causeway and is only an island at high tide. There was originally a chapel on the island but by the middle of the nineteenth century virtually all traces of it had disappeared. The present lighthouse was built in 1896 and decommissioned in 1994. It is now a museum and visitor centre and has a cafe.

Tel: 0191 200 8650

❶ From the car park, head towards the lighthouse and at a public footpath sign, turn sharp left up steps and continue along the winding coast path. On reaching the next car park, turn left along a tarmac drive to the A193 by the Delaval Arms, cross the main road and continue along the road opposite (Hartley Lane).

After 400m (0.25 miles), bear right ❷ along the tarmac drive to Hartley West Farm, cross a bridge over Seaton Burn and head uphill. At a public bridleway sign, bear left over a stile and continue along a path through Holywell Dene.

ⓘ This ancient wooded ravine follows the meanderings of Seaton Burn for about 8 km (5 miles) from Seghill, through Holywell village to Seaton Sluice where the burn flows into the North Sea.

ⓚ At the first fork take the left hand lower path and at the next one – a three way fork with a footbridge over the burn to the left – take the right hand uphill path to a T-junction and turn left to continue along the top right edge of the dene. Look out for a gate on the right, go through it and walk along the left edge of a field. Go through a hedge gap in the corner and as you continue along a track, the façade of Seaton Delaval Hall can be seen ahead.

Go through a gate, continue across fields, go through another gate and keep ahead along an enclosed path. Where a track joins from the left, pass beside a gate ahead and walk along the track by a row of cottages on the right (Harbord Terrace) to a road. **❸** Turn right for just over 400m (0.25 miles) to the entrance to Seaton Delaval Hall and a grand view of the north front.

Coastline near St Mary's Lighthouse

ⓘ Seaton Delaval Hall is one of the masterpieces of English Baroque architecture. It was designed by the renowned architect Sir John Vanbrugh – Blenheim Palace and Castle Howard are two of his other great houses – for Admiral George Delaval and was built between 1718 and 1728. It comprises a central block, flanked by two wings. The central block is in a semi-ruinous state, the west wing is still occupied and the east wing contains the stable block.

The house has had a chequered history. The Delaval line died out in the early nineteenth century and the house passed to the Astleys. In 1822 the central block was gutted by fire. As the Astleys were more interested in their estates in Norfolk and did not live at Seaton Delaval, the house was neglected and it was not until the 1860s that the central block was restored, and then only partially. It was more comprehensively restored in the 1960s and again at the end of the twentieth century by Edward Astley, 22nd Lord Hastings, and since the 1980s it has been occupied by the Astley family.

As well as the main house, there is a coach house and ice house and a stroll around the formal gardens is definitely to be recommended. Also worth visiting is the small Norman church near the house, built in 1102. It was originally the family chapel but was given to the local parish in 1891.

Tel: 0191 237 1493

🚶 **Retrace your steps along the road, continue past where you joined it and just beyond a turning on the right to New Hartley, turn left beside a gate at a public bridleway sign to Holywell. The straight enclosed track ahead follows the line of a former railway.**

ⓘ This was the Avenue Branch Railway Line, so called because it crossed the grand tree-lined avenue to Seaton Delaval Hall on its journey from the Northumberland

Holywell Dene

coalfield to the River Tyne. Originally it was a wooden waggonway along which horses pulled wooden coal trucks but in the nineteenth century it was converted to iron rails and steam-powered locomotives. It is one of a number of former waggonways in the area that have now become footpaths and cycle tracks.

After walking along the track for 1.6 km (1 mile), you re-enter Holywell Dene and pass under a disused railway bridge. Continue along the track, pass under another bridge and about 400m (0.25 miles) further on, turn left along an enclosed path at a Waggonways Cycle Route sign. ❹ To the right is the boundary of Whitley Bay golf course.

Seaton Delaval Hall

Seaton Delaval Hall

Where the path ends, turn left over a stile and
continue first along a tree-lined path and then along
the right edge of a field. Turn right over a ladder stile,
continue along the left field edge and in the corner,
turn left along an enclosed path by the edge of the golf
course again. Turn right to pass between the abutments
of a dismantled railway bridge and walk along an
enclosed path to the A193. Keep ahead and where the
road bends right, turn left along a tarmac drive to return
to the start.

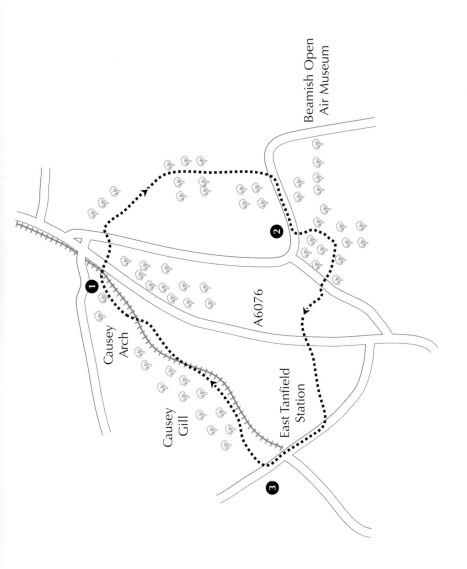

Beamish Open
Air Museum

Causey
Arch

Causey
Gill

A6076

East Tanfield
Station

WALK 7

Causey Arch

LENGTH:	6.4 km (4 miles)
TIME:	2 hours
TERRAIN:	Woodland and field paths, some gentle climbs, last stretch along the rim of a wooded gorge
START/PARKING:	Causey Arch, signposted from A6076 to the north of Stanley, GR NZ205562
BUS/TRAIN:	Buses from Consett and Stanley
REFRESHMENTS:	Pub near the start
MAP:	O.S. Explorer 308 – Durham & Sunderland

Fields, woodlands, sparkling streams and a dramatic gorge are the scenic ingredients of this walk on the edge of Gateshead. In view of its proximity to industrial Tyneside, it is not surprising that the chief historic interest is a monument and engineering triumph of the early Industrial Revolution; a railway bridge that carried coal trucks across the steep-sided Causey Gill.

❶ From the car park go under one of the two railway bridges to the A6076 and cross it to a public footpath sign. Turn left up an embankment to a stile, climb it and walk gently uphill along the right edge of a field. Climb a stile onto a lane, turn left and at a public footpath sign to Beamish Hall, turn sharp right along a hedge-lined track.

Causey Arch

Where the track bends right, keep ahead along a tree-lined path which later becomes a track. After passing beside a gate, the track continues through attractive woodland, heading down to a lane. Beamish Hall can be seen ahead.

❶ The seventeenth-century Beamish Hall is now a hotel. It lies next to the North of England Open Air Museum at Beamish. This fascinating museum shows life as it was in the area in the early 1900s and its numerous attractions include trams, steam engines, colliery village, railway station and farm. It is well worth a visit perhaps after completing the walk. Tel: 0191 370 4000

Ⓚ Turn right along the lane and at a public footpath sign, turn left ❷ along the drive to Beamishburn picnic area. Walk through the car park, keep ahead along a tarmac path and cross a footbridge over the burn. The path bends right and at a fork, take the right hand path to continue beside the burn. At a waymarked post, turn left uphill – steps in places – through Carrickshill Wood to a T-junction and turn right. Continue though the wood and at a junction of paths about 18m (20 yards) before reaching a barrier and lane, bear left and go through an arch in a wall onto the lane. Turn left uphill and at a public footpath sign to Causey Arch, turn right along an enclosed track.

Climb a stile, keep ahead quite steeply uphill and at a public footpath sign, turn left onto a narrower path. Climb another stile and continue uphill along the right edge of a field to a stile in the corner. After climbing it, turn right downhill, cross the A6076, climb the stile opposite and turn left uphill. The path curves right and continues to a stile. Climb it – and another one immediately ahead – head gently downhill along an enclosed path and climb a stile onto a road.

Cross over, turn right and at a public footpath sign to Causey Arch and the entrance to the Tanfield Railway, ❸ recross the road and walk along a wide track. Where the track bends right to the parking area for East Tanfield station, keep ahead along a path through a belt of trees. The path continues by the railway line and later Causey Burn on the right through the dramatic, steep-sided and thickly-wooded gorge of Causey Gill. Turn right to cross a footbridge over the burn, turn left and continue through this delightful woodland between the burn on the left and a railway embankment on the right. Bear right to cross the line and then turn left to continue along the right hand rim of the gorge.

Soon after seeing Causey Arch through the trees on the left, descend steps, recross the line and turn right along a tarmac path to the arch. From here there is a superb view of the gorge and you can descend steps to the bottom of it for a different perspective of the arch.

The Tanfield Railway is now a tourist attraction

🛈 The Causey Arch claims to be the oldest surviving single arch railway bridge in the world. It was built in 1725–26 by a group of local mine owners, called the 'Grand Allies', to carry the Tanfield Railway over the steep gorge of the Causey Burn. The railway originally had wooden rails and wooden horse-drawn wagons that transported coal from the pits around Stanley to the River Tyne. In the nineteenth century the wooden rails and horses were replaced by metal rails and steam locomotives.

Although of great historical and engineering significance, the arch had a brief working life. There were problems with landslips, Tanfield Colliery ceased production after an explosion in 1740 and other pits in the neighbourhood also closed down. By the 1770s it was virtually redundant, an alternative route was found and traffic over it ceased in 1786. At one time it was in danger of collapsing but restoration work in the 1970s and 80s enabled it to be saved as a striking monument to Britain's industrial history.

The railway line closed down in 1962 but later reopened as a tourist attraction. It carries passengers between Sunniside and East Tanfield and stops beside the Causey Arch. Appropriately a short stretch of wooden rail and a wooden coal truck is preserved at one end of the arch as a reminder of its origins. Tel: 0191 388 7545

🚶 **From the arch continue along a tarmac path parallel to the railway line and at a waymarked post, bear left and descend a flight of steps. At the bottom, bear right and head gently uphill passing beside a barrier to return to the start.**

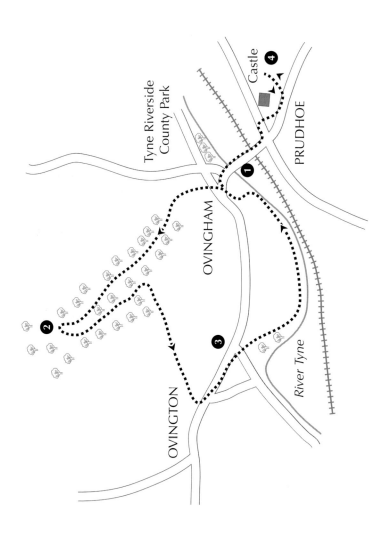

WALK 8

Ovingham, Overton and Prudhoe Castle

LENGTH:	8.9 km (5.5 miles)
TIME:	2.5 hours
TERRAIN:	Paths through a narrow wooded valley and along the edge of woodland, tracks, some road walking and a riverside path
START/PARKING:	Prudhoe, Tyne Riverside Country Park, GR NZ086635
BUS/TRAIN:	Buses and trains from Newcastle and Hexham
REFRESHMENTS:	Pubs at Prudhoe, pubs at Ovingham, restaurant/bar at Ovington
MAP:	O.S. Explorer 316 – Newcastle upon Tyne

Down by the River Tyne and railway station is called Low Prudhoe, the town centre is up on the hill and Prudhoe Castle is situated roughly half way between. The walk has plenty of both scenic and historic variety. It embraces a high level footbridge over the Tyne, an ancient church, two attractive villages, a lovely wooded dene, open views over the Tyne valley, pleasant riverside walking and a 'there and back' detour to the medieval castle.

❶ Tyne Riverside Country Park stretches intermittently along the banks of the Tyne from Newburn – on the western

Whittle Dene north of Ovingham

outskirts of Newcastle – through Wylam and onto Prudhoe, providing a series of pleasant, shady riverside walks. Some of it has been reclaimed from former industrial sites. At Prudhoe there is a visitor centre open at weekends and during school summer holidays.

❶ Begin by walking back to the road, turn left and cross the footbridge – parallel to the narrow road bridge – across the River Tyne into Ovingham. At a T-junction in front of the church, turn left and take the first lane on the right beside the churchyard wall.

The church at Ovingham is unusually interesting. It was founded in the eleventh century before the Norman

Conquest and the tall west tower survives from the original Anglo-Saxon building. Most of the rest of the church dates from a thirteenth-century rebuilding and is a fine example of the Early English Gothic style, with a number of narrow lancet windows.

🚶 **Follow the lane around a right bend and at a public footpath sign to Whittle Mill, Whittle Dene and Nafferton, climb steps and turn left over a stone stile. Walk along a track, climb a stile, keep ahead to go through a kissing gate and continue along a path. Ignore a flight of steps on the right and keep ahead to a gate. Go through, continue through a valley and the path enters the delightful woodland of Whittle Dene.**

Climb above Whittle Burn and continue through a grassy glade before plunging into woodland again, passing the remains of Whittle Mill, a former water-driven flour mill. At a path junction, keep along the lower path by the burn and after climbing above it again, the path descends to a footbridge. ❷ Turn left over it, go up steps – curving left – and climb above the other side of Whittle Burn. When you see a waymarked stile on the right, do not climb it but bear left to follow a path that keeps along the top inside edge of woodland, later emerging from the trees to continue along an enclosed path.

Head gently downhill and on reaching a track at a corner, turn right and follow it – the track is called St Andrew's Lane – into Ovington. In the village centre turn sharp left along a road and at a fork continue along the left hand lower road, heading downhill. Where a lane joins from the right, bear right, ❸ at a public footpath sign to River Tyne, along a tarmac track which continues gently downhill and at the bottom curves left beside the river.

Where the track bends left, keep ahead across grass to cross a footbridge and continue along a tree-lined riverside path. At one point a fine view of Prudhoe Castle

appears above the trees on the other side of the Tyne. Eventually the path curves left away from the river and widens into a track which emerges onto a road on the edge of Ovingham. Turn right into the village, passing the church again, and retrace your steps over the footbridge back into Prudhoe.

In order to visit the castle, keep ahead along the road over a level crossing and head up to a traffic island. Take the first turning on the left and after about 46m (50 yards), turn right up steps onto a higher road and turn left. The first turn on the left brings you to the castle entrance. ❹

ℹ️ Prudhoe Castle was built to guard a strategic crossing of the River Tyne and throughout its history it was involved in the many Anglo-Scottish conflicts. After a number of Scottish sieges, the stone keep, curtain walls and gatehouse were constructed towards the end of the twelfth century

River Tyne at Ovingham

Prudhoe Castle

and the castle was further strengthened in the thirteenth century. It was at this time that a chapel was built over the gatehouse.

It was originally owned by the Umfraville family but at the end of the fourteenth century it passed by marriage to the powerful Percys, later dukes of Northumberland. By the seventeenth century it had largely fallen into ruin but it still continued to be occupied and in the Georgian period a manor house was built on the site of some of the medieval buildings. Tel: 01833 638212

⊛ **From here retrace your steps back to the level crossing and turn left to return to the start.**

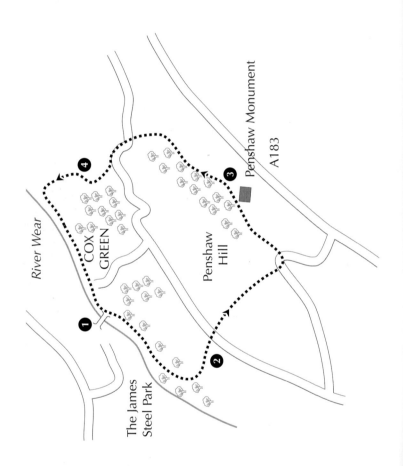

WALK 9

Penshaw Monument

LENGTH:	5.6 km (3.5 miles)
TIME:	1.5 hours
TERRAIN:	Riverside and woodland paths, steady climb up Penshaw Hill followed by quite a steep initial descent
START/PARKING:	The James Steel Park on the north side of the River Wear to the south east of Washington, follow signs to James Steel Park and Wetlands Centre from A1231 and at junction by the Asda Distribution Centre turn left, in the James Steel Park and Riverside direction, to reach the car park at a footbridge over the river, GR NZ325554
BUS/TRAIN:	None
REFRESHMENTS:	Pub at Cox Green
MAP:	O.S. Explorer 308 – Durham & Sunderland

The opening and closing sections of the walk are along attractive wooded riverside paths beside the River Wear. In between you climb the slopes of Penshaw Hill, 136m (446 feet) high, to a grand Victorian monument, visible for miles around and a magnificent 360 degree viewpoint.

ℹ The James Steel Park stretches for almost 4 km (2.5 miles) along both banks of the River Wear between the Wetlands Centre in the east and Fatfield Bridge in the west. It is named after James Steel who was Lord Lieutenant of Tyne and Wear from 1974 to 1984 and also served as Chairman of Washington Development Corporation. Once the scene of industrial activity with wharves, warehouses and shipbuilding yards, it is now a peaceful waterside area fringed by woodland.

❶ Begin by crossing the footbridge over the River Wear into the hamlet of Cox Green and turn right along the riverside path. Go through a kissing gate and continue along an enclosed path through woodland. The path later bears slightly left away from the river and heads gently uphill. Ahead is the striking but now disused Victoria Viaduct.

At a waymarked post in front of the viaduct, turn left and continue gently uphill through a lovely wooded valley to a stile. Climb it, turn sharp left along a track, turn right in front of a row of cottages and continue along a path which heads up to a stile. Climb it, turn right, walk across a field – the former field boundary can just about be seen – and on the far side go up steps and cross a track to a road. ❷ Cross over, climb a stile and head uphill along the right edge of a field. Look out for where you bear slightly right through a gap to continue along the left field edge and climb another stile onto a road.

Turn left, follow the road around a right bend and at a public footpath sign to Penshaw Hill, turn left along an enclosed track. Pass beside a gate, keep ahead gently uphill to a junction of paths and tracks and bear left up steps and through woodland to a kissing gate. Go through, ascend some steps and turn right off the path to go up more steps to the Penshaw Monument on top of the hill. ❸

ℹ At a height of 136m (446 feet), the Penshaw Monument
is a magnificent all round viewpoint. The immediate
surroundings are urban and industrial but the views extend
out to sea, westwards to the Durham Dales and north
Pennines and in clear conditions, the line of the Cheviots
can be seen on the northern horizon.

The monument looks like a blackened version of
the Parthenon in Athens transported to the outskirts of
Sunderland and in fact its design is based on that of an
Athenian temple. It is 30m (100 feet) long, 16m (53 feet)
wide and 20m (70 feet) high and comprises 18 huge Doric
columns. It was built in 1844 in honour of John George

River Wear near Cox Green

The Penshaw Monument, a landmark for miles around

Lambton, Earl of Durham and first Governor-General of Canada. In 1939 one of his successors presented it to the National Trust who subsequently acquired the adjacent woodland as well.

ⓧ **From the monument, turn left and head down a grassy embankment to rejoin the main path at a kissing gate. Go through and keep ahead along the top inside edge of sloping woodland, climbing several stiles. Later the route continues along a left field edge to a stile. After climbing it, immediately turn left and head steeply downhill to another stile. Climb it, continue downhill across the next field and climb a stile onto a lane.**

Turn left, cross a bridge over a disused railway track and keep ahead along what is now a tarmac drive which bends to the right. Where the drive bends right again towards a golf club car park, climb a stile in front ❹ and walk along a tree-lined path which descends to the banks of the Wear. Turn left onto a riverside path, go through a kissing gate and continue into Cox Green. Pass the pub, keep ahead to the footbridge and turn right over it to return to the start.

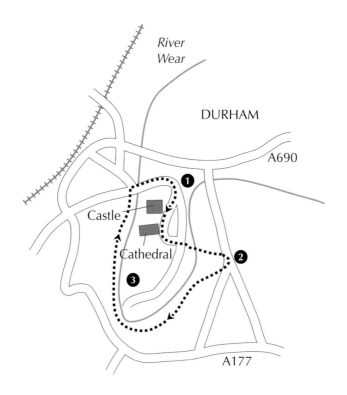

*River
Wear*

DURHAM

A690

Castle

Cathedral

A177

WALK 10

Historic Durham

LENGTH:	3.2 km (2 miles)
TIME:	1 hour
TERRAIN:	Combination of lovely old streets and wooded riverside paths
START/PARKING:	Durham, Market Place, GR NZ274425. Pay car parks at Durham
BUS/TRAIN:	Buses from Newcastle, Darlington, Sunderland, Hartlepool and all the surrounding towns; trains from Newcastle and Darlington
REFRESHMENTS:	Plenty of pubs, restaurants, wine bars and coffee shops in Durham
MAP:	O.S. Explorer 308 – Durham & Sunderland

In his iconic series 'The Buildings of England', Pevsner described Durham as 'one of the great experiences of Europe to the eyes of those who appreciate architecture, and to the minds of those who understand architecture' and few would disagree with this assessment after completing this short but fascinating walk. The combination of cathedral, castle and other picturesque old buildings, crammed into a horseshoe bend of the River Wear and towering above wooded riverside paths, creates a uniquely memorable walk. The suggested time of 1 hour is purely academic as you will inevitably want to linger and take in the magnificent views and soak in the atmosphere of this beautiful city.

The classic view of Durham Cathedral

(🚶) ❶ **From the Market Place begin by walking up Saddler Street, signposted to Cathedral and Castle. At a fork take the right hand upper street and turn right up Owengate to Palace Green. Ahead is the cathedral and to the right is the castle.**

ⓘ The sight of the cathedral and castle rising majestically side by side on the steep cliff overlooking the River Wear is unrivalled. These buildings reveal more clearly than any words the immense powers, both spiritual and temporal, exercised by the medieval bishops of Durham. They were princes as well as churchmen, responsible for the defence of this part of England against Scottish raids as well as for the administration of their diocese.

Durham Cathedral is undoubtedly one of the great buildings of Europe. Originally founded in 995 to house the remains of St Cuthbert, the cathedral was built mainly between 1093 and 1133 and is regarded as a masterpiece of Norman architecture. The massive columns of the nave, characterised by the differing patterns on the stonework, are particularly impressive. Unusually the Lady Chapel, added around 1170 and known as the Galilee Chapel, was placed at the west end of the church rather than the east end. It contains the tomb of the Venerable Bede, a monk from nearby Jarrow who has been described as the 'Father of English History'. The cathedral is almost entirely in the Norman style apart from the fortress-looking thirteenth-century Chapel of the Nine Altars at the east end, the upper parts of the twin west towers and the imposing central tower, the latter built in the late fifteenth century. Tel: 0191 386 4266

Durham Castle dates from the late eleventh century and despite extensive rebuilding and extensions over the centuries, it still retains the basic plan of a simple motte and bailey castle. It was the chief residence and stronghold of the prince bishops until 1832 when it was given to the newly founded University of Durham and converted into a residential college. More alterations took place to enable it to fulfil its new role, during which the ruined Norman keep was restored. Tel: 0191 334 3800

(⊛) **In the far left corner of Palace Green turn left along a cobbled path (Dun Cow Lane) to the church of St Mary-le-Bow.**

(ⓘ) The small medieval church of St Mary-le-Bow was largely rebuilt in the late seventeenth century. Now redundant, it houses the Durham Heritage Centre which tells the story

of the city from its tenth-century origins to the present day.
Tel: 0191 384 5589

🚶 **Turn right and immediately turn left beside the church
down Bow Lane and cross the modern Kingsgate
footbridge, built in 1963, which soars high over the River
Wear. On the other side turn right along Church Street
❷ and at a footpath sign to Riverside, bear right across
the churchyard of St Oswald's – not on the paved path
that leads up to the church but along the rough path to
the right of it.**

🛈 St Oswalds's is one of a number of medieval churches
within the city. It was built in the late twelfth century,
enlarged in the thirteenth century and the tower was added
in the fifteenth century. The church was almost demolished
in the Victorian period but was saved by the determined
action of its parishioners.

🚶 **At a fork take the right hand lower path down to the
Wear. Continue through the delightful woods beside the
river, following it around a right bend to reach Prebends
Bridge. ❸**

🛈 The graceful Prebends Bridge was built in 1777 and from
here you can enjoy the first of a succession of memorable
views of Durham Cathedral – and later the castle – above
the steep, wooded banks of the Wear. These views are
among the greatest visual experiences in Britain and have
inspired, among others, the landscape painter JMW Turner
and the Scottish writer and poet Sir Walter Scott. Scott's
famous lines are inscribed at the western end of the bridge:
'Grey towers of Durham, yet well I love thy mixed and
massive piles, half church of God, half castle 'gainst the
Scot, and long to roam these venerable aisles with records
stored of deeds long since forgot'.

The cathedral and castle at Durham from Prebends Bridge

Ⓚ **Continue along the riverside path to the fifteenth-century Framwellgate Bridge and in front of it, go up steps and turn right over it. Continue along Silver Street, heading up to the starting point in the Market Place.**

Durham Castle

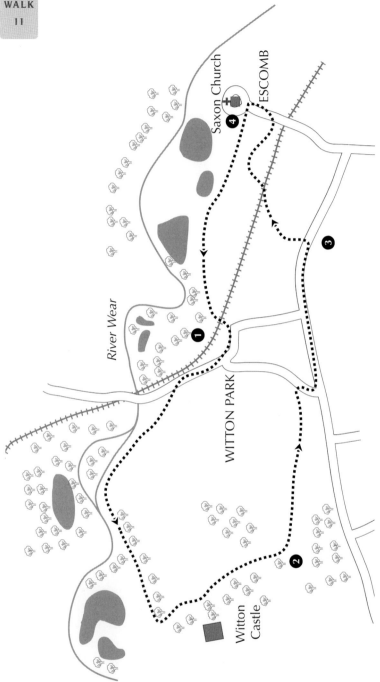

WALK 11

Wear Valley and Escomb

LENGTH:	8.9 km (5.5 miles)
TIME:	2.5 hours
TERRAIN:	About 1.2 km (0.75 miles) of road walking, otherwise mainly paths and tracks across gently undulating countryside
START/PARKING:	Witton Park, on the south side of the River Wear between Bishop Auckland and the A68, follow signs to Paradise car park at the bottom (northern) end of the village, GR NZ174304
BUS/TRAIN:	Buses from Bishop Auckland
REFRESHMENTS:	Pub at Escomb
MAP:	O.S. Explorer 305 – Bishop Auckland

Once this area of the Wear valley was in the heart of the Durham coalfield but now the collieries and their attendant waste tips have been replaced by pleasant woodland, parkland and lakes. The focal point of the walk is a visit to the Saxon church at Escomb. From many points there are fine and extensive views across the valley.

❶ From the car park follow the track back to the village and at a crossroads just after passing under a railway bridge, turn right. Follow the road around a right bend, keep ahead and at a public footpath sign Wearside Way,

turn left over a stile and walk along a gently ascending
track.

After climbing a stile, walk across a field, climb a stile
at the far narrowing end and continue along a tree-lined
track by woodland on the right that slopes down to the
River Wear. Where the track curves left, keep ahead to
climb a stile in the field corner and continue through
woodland above the river. The path later descends to
keep briefly beside the river – here you have to negotiate
a short stretch across boulders – before re-entering
woodland. Look out for a footpath post at a fork where
you take the left hand path and continue along right edge
of Holme Wood by a stream on the left.

The path becomes enclosed and goes up steps and
through a squeezer stile onto another path. Turn left and
head uphill along this enclosed path. Over the wall on
the right occasional glimpses of Witton Castle can be
seen through the trees.

River Wear near Witton Park

Looking over the Wear Valley from near Witton Castle

1 Witton Castle dates mainly from the fourteenth and fifteenth centuries with later additions and amendments. Set in woodland, it is now the focal point of a camping and caravan site.

The path later widens into a track and after nearly 1.2 km (0.75 miles), turn left over a stile at a crossways ❷ and walk along the right edge of a field. After climbing two stiles in quick succession, the way continues along left field edges and later along a right field edge again. Finally after an enclosed path and track you reach a road at the top (southern) end of Witton Park village. Turn right and at a T-junction turn left. Head down into a dip and up again and after about 1.2 km (0.75 miles), turn left through a kissing gate, at a public footpath sign, ❸ and head downhill along an enclosed path.

 Go through a kissing gate, bear right, continue gently downhill across a field, go through another kissing gate

and keep in the same direction across the next field. After the next kissing gate, the way continues along an enclosed path above a railway line on the left. Go through a gate, turn left to cross a footbridge over the railway line, keep ahead along a track which bends right and follow this wide track across a recreation ground, curving first right and then left.

ⓘ The recreation ground is on the site of the George Pit which opened in 1837 and closed in 1924. Between those years it was the chief source of employment in the area.

🚶 **On emerging onto a road in Escomb, turn left downhill through the village to the Saxon church.**

ⓘ How much conditions have changed here in the past half century can be gauged from Pevsner's comment in the County Durham volume of his monumental 'Buildings of England' series. Writing in the 1950s he described the church as lying amidst 'desperately sordid surroundings' Now the location of this highly atmospheric building at the bottom end of the small village can be summed up with adjectives such as pleasant and attractive.

Escomb is one of the oldest churches in the country and a rare example of a surviving Saxon church. Typically small and narrow, it was built in the late seventh century and the quality of the stonework suggests that some of the stones came from the nearby Roman fort at Binchester. Among its outstanding features are a late seventh or early eighth century Saxon sundial on the external south wall, some of the original Saxon windows and the fine chancel arch, again possibly of Roman origin and brought from Binchester.

🚶 **In front of the church, turn left ❹ to pass in front of the Saxon Inn and where the road ends, keep ahead along a** track, rejoining the Weardale Way for the remainder of the walk. Where the track bends right, go through a gate and walk along a path to a kissing gate. Go through that, keep ahead across a field, go through a hedge gap and continue across the next field, heading down into a dip where you climb a waymarked stile.

Continue up by the right edge of a field, climb a stile and walk across a young plantation to another stile. After climbing it, keep ahead along an enclosed path, go through a gate and head down a track towards the railway bridge near the start of the walk. Turn right in front of it to return to the car park.

Saxon church at Escomb

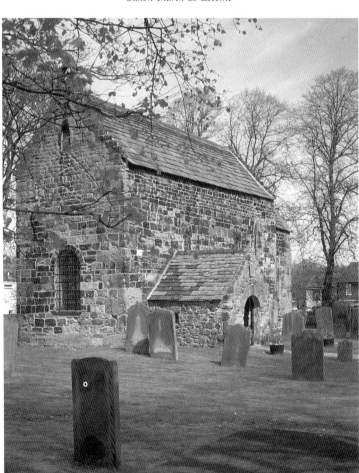

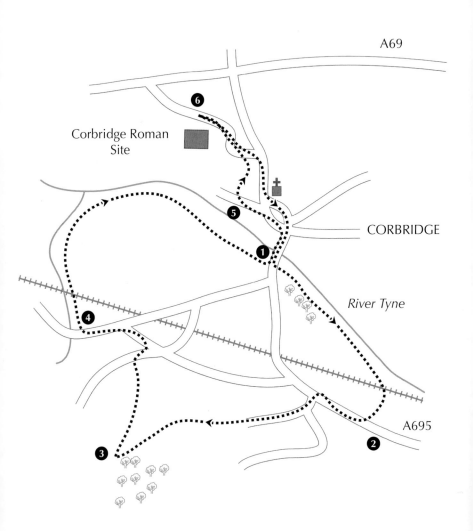

A69

Corbridge Roman
Site

6

✝

5

1

CORBRIDGE

River Tyne

4

2

A695

3

BLACK BULL (CHEF + BREWER)

GOOD REVIEWS

WALK 12

Both Banks of the River Tyne at Corbridge

LENGTH:	11.3 km (7 miles)
TIME:	3.5 hours
TERRAIN:	Mainly along easy riverside, woodland and field paths
START/PARKING:	Pay car park on south side of the bridge at Corbridge, GR NY988641
BUS/TRAIN:	Buses and trains from Newcastle and Hexham
REFRESHMENTS:	Pubs and tea shops in Corbridge
MAP:	O.S. Explorer OL43 – Hadrian's Wall

The interest is chiefly scenic on the first part of this figure of eight walk around Corbridge; the historic interest comes on the second – shorter – circuit. Initially you explore some of the attractive countryside on the south side of the River Tyne, with pleasant riverside walking and fine views. After returning to the starting point, you visit the Roman site to the west of the present village before walking through the village centre, passing the old church and a building that is a reminder of the border warfare that once plagued this area.

ⓘ The original bridge over the River Tyne at Corbridge was built in 1235. As a result of frequent floods, it had become ruinous by the seventeenth century and the present handsome structure was built in 1674 and widened in the late nineteenth century.

❶ Cross the road by the end of the bridge and take the path opposite. Immediately climb a stone stile and take the riverside path through woodland, later continuing along the top of an embankment. When adjacent to the railway line, look out for a stile on the right. Climb it, go up steps, carefully cross the railway line, go up steps on the other side and climb another stile.

Keep ahead uphill through woodland, curving left to ascend a long flight of steps. Climb a stile at the top, bear right along the right edge of a field and go through a gate onto a road. ❷ Turn right, take the first road on the left (signposted to Temperley Grange) and turn right along a lane at a public footpath sign to Ladycutter Lane. To the right are attractive views of Corbridge and the

Corbridge from the River Tyne and opposite,
The Vicar's Pele at Corbridge, a mini-castle

Remains of the Roman settlement of Corstopitum near Corbridge

Tyne valley. Where the lane – now more of a tarmac
track – bends left at the entrance to West Fell, keep
ahead along an enclosed path to a gate. Go through,
keep ahead to go through two more gates and where the
path bends left, turn right through another gate. ❸ The
next part of the route is along a permissive bridleway and
is part of a Conservation Walk.

Walk along the right edge of a field, go through a
gate and when about half-way along the edge of the next
field, turn right through a metal gate and turn left along
a track to a road. Turn right, at a T-junction turn left and
at the next T-junction turn left again. At a public footpath
sign to Corbridge – just before Dilston Bridge – turn right

❹ down steps and go through a kissing gate.

Walk along an enclosed path above Devil's Water and go up steps to carefully cross the railway line again. Descend steps and continue by the stream, bearing right on joining a track to reach the confluence of Devil's Water and the River Tyne. Keep by the river to return to the bridge at Corbridge. ❶

For the second – shorter and more urban – part of the figure-of-eight, cross the bridge into the village and immediately turn sharp left down steps at a public footpath sign Riverside. Walk along a pleasant riverside path and on emerging into a clearing, bear right across the grass to a tarmac track. ❺ Turn left and at a

Corstopitum lay at the junction of two major Roman roads and was a site of some significance

public bridleway sign to Stagshaw Road, turn right onto an enclosed path. Follow the path as it bends right between houses and turn left along another enclosed path between garden fences on the left and a wall on the right. The path curves left, heads gently uphill and widens out to reach a road.

Turn left and follow the road around right and left bends to reach the entrance to the Roman site. ❻

ℹ The Roman site at Corbridge (Corstopitum) lies at the junction of two important routes, the Stanegate running from east to west and Dere Street running from north to south. It has had a varied history with four forts and a town occupying the site.

It lies about 3.6 km (2.25 miles) to the south of Hadrian's Wall but the first two forts here, built in the late first and early second centuries AD predate it. The third fort was built roughly at the same time as the building of the wall probably to serve as a back-up and supply fort housing infantry troops. The fort was partially rebuilt again when the frontier was temporarily moved northwards to the Antonine Wall in Scotland but when Hadrian's Wall was reinstated, the number of forts on the wall itself seems to have made Corbridge redundant. Most of the buildings of the fort were demolished and by the beginning of the third century it had developed into more of a civilian town but still with a garrison and a reduced military role.

Most of the remaining buildings date from this later period when it was a town but there are still the foundations of the headquarters building and commandant's house from the earlier forts. Although the site is extensive, most of it still lies unexcavated under the adjacent fields. There are impressive remains of temples, granaries, workshops, houses and barracks and a wide range of artefacts dug up from the site in the museum that illustrate the many different aspects of life, work, recreation and death in the Roman town. In particular look out for the Corbridge Lion, a sculpture of a lion crouching over a stag, later used as an ornamental fountain head. Tel: 01434 632349

🚶 **Retrace your steps along the road and keep along it to a T-junction. Turn right, follow the road into the centre of the village and turn left into the Market Place.**

❶ The Market Place is dominated by the imposing church, a mixture of styles. There has been a church on the site since the seventh century and some of the original Saxon work remains in the west tower. It also has a Norman doorway but most of it dates from the thirteenth century and was restored in Victorian times.

Nearby on the south side of the churchyard is the fourteenth-century Vicar's Pele Tower. Pele towers were small fortified towers, sort of mini-castles, built all over the border counties as protection against frequent raids from across the Scottish border. A few can be found as far south as Lancashire but most of them were in Cumbria, Durham and Northumberland. Some were small manor houses, some were attached to isolated farms but it is unusual to find one built as a vicarage. It had three storeys: the ground floor housed animals and was used for storage, the first floor was the living area and the vicar would retire to the top floor at a time of danger. It continued in use until as late as the early seventeenth century.

🚶 **Continue along Middle Street and turn right down to the bridge. Cross it to return to the start.**

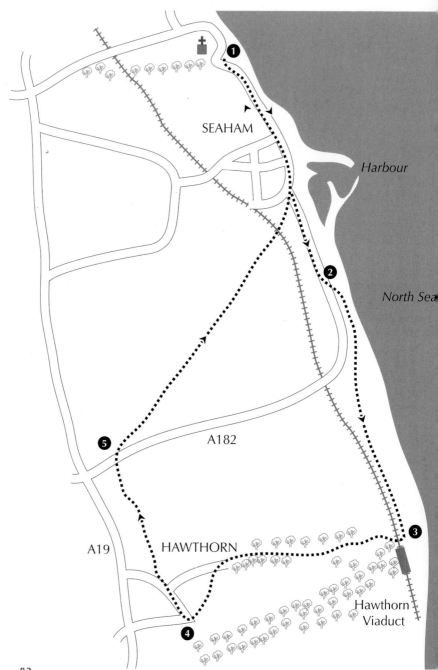

SEAHAM

Harbour

North Sea

②

③

A182

⑤

A19

HAWTHORN

④

Hawthorn
Viaduct

①

WALK 13

Durham Coast near Seaham

LENGTH:	12.9 km (8 miles)
TIME:	4 hours
TERRAIN:	Fairly flat walking on coast and woodland paths, last 3.2 km (2 miles) mostly along a former railway track
START/PARKING:	Seaham, follow signs for Seafront from the B1404, do not use the large car park where the road bends right on reaching the coast but the next one about 400m (0.25 miles) further on near St Mary's church, GR NZ426505
REFRESHMENTS:	Pubs and cafes at Seaham, pub at Hawthorn
BUS/TRAIN:	Buses from Newcastle, Sunderland, Durham, Darlington and Middlesbrough; trains from Newcastle, Sunderland, Hartlepool and Middlesbrough
MAP:	O.S. Explorer 308 – Durham & Sunderland

The walk is all about reclamation and regeneration, transforming industrial eyesores into something like the areas of natural beauty that they were before the Industrial Revolution. This stretch of the Durham coast was a mining coast with collieries, industrial sites and waste tips on the actual cliff tops and coal washed up onto the beaches. Now it has once again become an attractive coastline, backed by pleasant and unspoilt countryside inland, although much of the latter always remained relatively unscathed by the nearby collieries. Enjoy this fascinating route through a post-industrial landscape of limestone cliffs and grassland, sandy beaches, deep valleys and beautiful areas of woodland.

ℹ️ Seaham is a town in transition, attempting to transform itself from a decayed Victorian mining town and redundant coal port into a modern retail centre and resort. One of its advantages is the fine sandy beaches and new buildings are springing up all over the place, many of them on old colliery sites. At the height of the mining industry there were three pits in the town – Seaham, Dawdon and Vane Tempest – as well as others in the locality but these had all closed down by the 1990s.

Before the coming of the collieries, Seaham was a small coastal settlement to the north of the present town centre, based around the fine medieval church of St Mary, across the road from near where the walk begins. Close to the church is Seaham Hall, built in the late eighteenth century and now a luxury hotel and spa. Its main claim to fame is that Lord Byron married Annabella Milbanke, the daughter of the owner, here in 1815.

🚶 **❶ With the sea on your left, walk along the road above the beach towards Seaham town centre. On the other side of the road you see some of the new housing built on the site of the Vane Tempest Colliery and further on you pass some impressive nineteenth-century buildings around the harbour.**

Continue along the coast road (signposted Docks and A182) and approaching a road junction just beyond the Seaham Docks and Harbour Building, follow the path as it curves left ❷ away from the main roads and traffic. As the path keeps along the grassy cliff top, there are

extensive views along the coast from Sunderland in the north to Hartlepool in the south, with the line of the Cleveland Hills visible on the southern horizon in clear weather.

ⓘ The Durham coast was previously one of the most polluted coastlines in Britain, devastated by coal mines, industrial installations and waste tips. Following the closure of the last of the pits, an extensive project was undertaken between 1997 and 2002 to clean it up, restore it to something approaching its former appearance and make it a recreational asset to locals and visitors alike. The major task was to remove the tons of colliery waste and debris. The spoil tips were landscaped, covered with soil and grassed over to create limestone meadows and a continuous footpath was created running along the coast from Seaham to Crimdon Dene. So successful was this reclamation programme that in 2001 Durham was designated a Heritage Coast, on a par with any elsewhere in Britain.

⍟ **Walk past the promontory of Noses Point and continue through a car park, which occupies the site of the former Dawdon Colliery. After keeping above Blast Beach, the path now continues along the right edge of the cliff tops and later alongside a railway line on the right. At a railway bridge, descend some steps and keep ahead along the right field edge to enter woodland and reach a bay by the headland of Chourdon Point. Turn right over a stile, ❸ carefully cross the railway line, climb another stile and take the path ahead across Hawthorn Dene Meadows – a rare and fine example of limestone grassland.**

At this point you can make a brief detour along the first path on the left, go through a kissing gate and descend steps into Hawthorn Dene.

ⓘ Hawthorn Dene is one of a number of denes or deep
wooded valleys that cut into the Durham coastline. An
impressive Victorian railway viaduct carries the line from
Sunderland to Hartlepool across its mouth.

🚶 **Return to the main route, turn left on rejoining it but
almost immediately turn right onto another path. Turn
left in front of a gate and follow a delightful path
through the exceptionally attractive woodlands of New
Plantation and Haythorne's Plantation. From time to time
there are superb views looking across the fields on the
left to Hawthorn Dene. Later continue along the top
inside edge of the trees and after passing beside a barrier,
keep ahead along an enclosed path to a lane.**

The sandy beach at Seaham

Blast Beach near Seaham, once an ugly industrial eyesore on this stretch of the Durham coast

Turn left and at a public footpath sign, turn left again along a tree-lined path. Cross a footbridge over a burn, keep ahead and pass beside a barrier onto a track. Turn right – the track later becomes a tarmac one – and by the Stapylton Arms, turn right ❹ along a road through the small village of Hawthorn. At a road junction, keep ahead along a tree-lined track and after passing a large house on the left, the track narrows to a path which continues in a straight line across a succession of fields. On the far side of the last field, go through a gap and turn left along an enclosed path. Follow the path around a right bend, climb a stile and keep ahead along a track. Cross a tarmac track, continue on to pass beside a barrier and carefully cross the busy A182.

Pass beside another barrier opposite and almost immediately turn right onto a tarmac track, ❺ a former railway line that linked some of the East Durham pits with Seaham Harbour. Follow the track for 3.2 km (2 miles) back to Seaham. The track is tree-lined at times and in the latter stages there are fine views over Seaham and along a broad sweep of the coast looking towards Sunderland.

After passing under a road bridge, continue beside a road on the right, pass under two railway bridges and finally the track emerges onto a road. Keep ahead, bear right on joining another road and follow it to the left into Seaham town centre. On rejoining the coast road retrace your steps to the start.

Beautiful woodland near Hawthorn

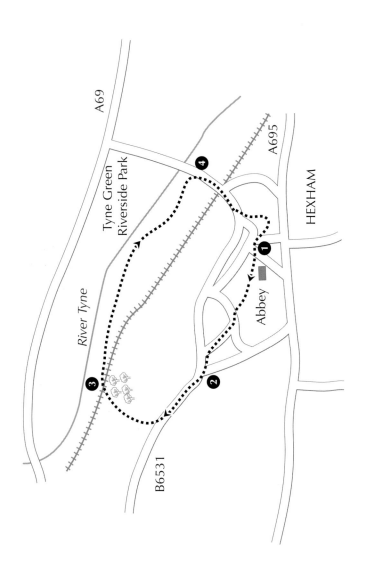

A69

A695

HEXHAM

Tyne Green
Riverside Park

River Tyne

Abbey

B6531

WALK 14

Around Hexham

LENGTH:	4.8 km (3 miles)
TIME:	1.5 hours
TERRAIN:	Easy town walking, plus a tree-lined track and riverside path
START/PARKING:	Hexham, Market Place, GR NY936642. A choice of pay car parks in Hexham, including the large Wentworth car park just a short walk from the Market Place
BUS/TRAIN:	Buses from Newcastle, Consett and Morpeth; trains from Newcastle
REFRESHMENTS:	Plenty of tea shops, restaurants and pubs in the centre of Hexham
MAP:	O.S. Explorer OL43 – Hadrian's Wall

From the centre of Hexham this short and easy walk passes the major historic buildings in the town and takes you across some of the green areas that are one of its most attractive features. Particularly pleasant is the tree-lined stretch beside the River Tyne.

❶ **Start in the Market Place and facing the east end of the abbey, take the path to the right of it.**

❶ Hexham Abbey is one of the most ancient Christian sites in northern England It was founded by St Wilfrid in 674 as a Benedictine abbey and was for a time the seat of

The Moot Hall overlooks the Market Place at Hexham

a Northumbrian bishopric. Of the original Saxon church the crypt remains, a rare surviving example of Saxon architecture in a major church.

The Normans converted the Saxon abbey into an Augustinian priory. Following the dissolution of the monasteries by Henry VIII and Thomas Cromwell in the 1530s, most of the monastic buildings were destroyed but the priory church survived and became the parish church. The church was mostly built in the late twelfth and early thirteenth centuries and is a fine example of Early English Gothic. By the middle of the nineteenth century it had fallen into a state of disrepair, necessitating the rebuilding of the east end in 1860 and the nave in 1908.

The path becomes a road (Cowgarth) and later a tarmac track which runs along the right edge of a recreation ground.

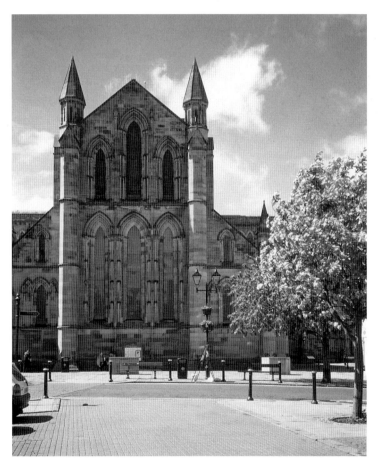 Hexham is fortunate in that there are a number of adjacent green spaces on the western side of the town centre. These include the grounds of the early eighteenth-century

Hexham Abbey

Hexham House, the landscaped Abbey Grounds which boast a Victorian bandstand, and The Sele. The word 'sele' is an Old English name for hall and there may have been a hall on this site during the Anglo-Saxon period. In the Middle Ages it belonged to the canons of the abbey and later came into the ownership of the lord of the manor. It has been a public recreation area for over 250 years.

At a fork – just after passing a school on the right – take the right hand downhill path and cross a footbridge over a stream onto a road. Turn left and at a fork take the right hand road (Millfield Terrace), heading up to a T-junction. Turn left to a crossroads and turn right.

Hexham Abbey

River Tyne at Hexham

❷ After nearly 800m (0.5 miles) turn right, at a public
bridleway sign to Tyne Green, along a tarmac track which
heads downhill across a golf course. At a fork continue
downhill along the left hand tree-lined track, signposted
to Spittal Lane, and the track later narrows to a path
which descends to a tarmac track.

Immediately turn left over a stone stile, carefully
cross a railway line, go through a gate and turn right. ❸
You now follow a delightful route through Tyne Green
Country Park beside the tree-lined banks of the Tyne,
eventually emerging onto a road. ❹

Bridge over the River Tyne at Hexham

ⓘ Tyne Green Country Park was given to the people of Hexham in 1887 to commemorate the Golden Jubilee of Queen Victoria and became a country park in 1982. This lovely green area stretches for about 3.2 km (2 miles) along the banks of the River Tyne.

🚶 **Turn right, cross a railway bridge and turn left to walk across Wentworth car park to the tourist information centre at the far end. Turn right up steps and continue along Hallgate, passing the Old Gaol and passing under the arch of the Moot Hall to return to the Market Place.**

❶ After the abbey the Old Gaol and Moot Hall are Hexham's principal historic buildings. Both were originally part of the complex of buildings that made up the Archbishop's Hall, the medieval residence of the archbishops of York who were lords of the manor of Hexham. The Old Gaol, recently restored as a museum, was built in the fourteenth century and was used as a prison until 1824.

The Moot Hall was built as the gatehouse to the Archbishop's Hall and was heavily fortified because of the danger of Scottish raids. It later was used as a court house.

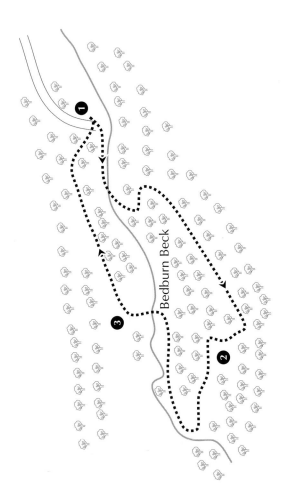

WALK 15

Hamsterley Forest

LENGTH:	6.4 km (4 miles)
TIME:	2 hours
TERRAIN:	Forest tracks and paths, modest climbs
START/PARKING:	Hamsterley Forest Visitor Centre, follow signs to Hamsterley and Hamsterley Forest from A68 to the south of Witton-le-Wear, parking is free but you have to pay to use the Forest Toll Road in order to get there, GR NY093314
BUS/TRAIN:	None
REFRESHMENTS:	Tearoom by the Visitor Centre
MAP:	Explorer OL31 – North Pennines – Teesdale & Weardale

A walk through Hamsterley Forest finds a place in a book of historic walks because it is one of the more recent additions to the landscape of north east England. Begun in the 1920s, it extends over a large area on both sides of the valley of Bedburn Beck and its mixture of conifer plantations, deciduous trees, steep slopes and open grassland has become a popular and well-established recreational asset. The walk is easy to follow, using an orange-coded route on the first leg and switching to a yellow-coded route later.

🛈 Hamsterley Forest, the largest forest in County Durham covering around 2000 hectares, was one of a number of commercial forests established in the years after World War I. By the end of the war Britain's timber resources had been so severely depleted that the Forestry Commission was set up with the task of remedying that problem. Throughout the country large numbers of fast-growing conifers were planted, both in existing forests and in new, previously non-wooded parts of the country in the 1920s and 30s.

Hamsterley Forest

Hamsterley had previously been a hunting estate. Planting began in 1927 and helped to provide much needed work for local unemployed miners and other jobless workers during the worst years of the Great Depression. Although primarily planted for commercial reasons, these new forests were to develop a recreational role and Hamsterley is no exception. Car parks, a forest drive and colour-coded cycle trails and walking routes, plus a visitor centre and tearoom, have all helped to make the forest a hugely popular weekend and bank holiday destination for local people. But the major reason for its popularity is of course the stunning scenery, beautiful woodland paths, sparkling burns and sense of remoteness and solitude.

❶ In front of the visitor centre, descend steps, walk across the car park and turn right onto a well-surfaced path beside the delightful Bedburn Beck. Turn left to cross a bridge over the beck, head gently uphill along a track and at a junction, turn right.

At the next orange waymark, turn right onto a steeply ascending path to reach a track and turn right. Cross a road, head gently uphill along a path and at an orange waymark where the main path curves left, turn right downhill to emerge onto a track. ❷ Turn right – here leaving the orange-coded route – and after a few yards, turn left, at a blue-waymarked post, onto a short stretch of path to a road. Turn left downhill back into the valley of Bedburn Beck and at the bottom, bear right onto a track, here joining the yellow-coded route for the remainder of the walk. Continue downhill and at a junction of tracks, turn right and walk by the right bank of the beck.

At a fork take the right hand path which climbs gently through the trees, giving some grand views over the forest. Look out for where a yellow waymark directs you

Hamsterley Forest

to turn left quite steeply downhill to cross a footbridge over the beck. Keep ahead across grass to the forest road and turn right.

Cross a beck and at a fork, ❸ take the left hand uphill road. At a waymarked post, bear right along a most attractive wooded path to a T-junction and turn right. Head gently downhill, descend a short flight of steps to the road and turn left to return to the visitor centre.

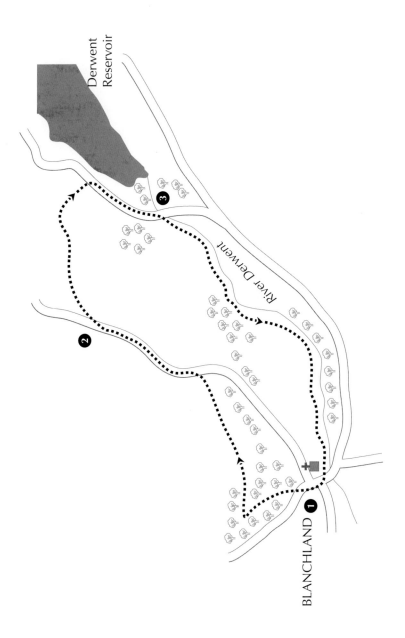

Derwent
Reservoir

River Derwent

BLANCHLAND

WALK 16

Blanchland and Derwent Reservoir

LENGTH:	8 km (5 miles)
TIME:	2.5 hours
TERRAIN:	Well-signed paths and tracks through woodland, across fields and by a river, some road walking and one climb at the start
START/PARKING:	Free car park at Blanchland on the north side of the village, GR NY965505
BUS/TRAIN:	Buses from Consett
REFRESHMENTS:	Pub and cafe at Blanchland
MAP:	O.S. Explorer 307 – Consett & Derwent Reservoir or O.S. Explorer OL43 – Hadrian's Wall

From the pretty village of Blanchland, built on the site of a medieval abbey, an initial climb through woodland leads out onto a hillside with glorious views over Derwent Reservoir. The route continues down into the Derwent valley and the final leg is along wooded riverside paths. The River Derwent here is the county boundary between Northumberland and Durham.

🛈 Blanchland is a monastic village, gloriously situated on the north bank of the River Derwent and surrounded by steep

wooded slopes and open moorland. Most of it is built on
the site of a medieval monastery: the parish church is a
small part of the original abbey church, the Lord Crewe
Arms occupies the Abbot's Lodgings, many of the cottages
are built on the foundations of the domestic buildings
around the abbey cloister and most of the village structures
incorporate some of the former monastic buildings.

The abbey belonged to the Premonstratensian Order
and was founded in 1165. It was partially destroyed by the
Scots in 1327 and closed down by Henry VIII in the 1530s.
All that is left of the abbey church is the tower, north
transept and choir which in 1753 were converted into the
present parish church.

The picturesque village of Blanchland is built on the site of a medieval abbey

The church at Blanchland, converted from the remains of the abbey

Overlooking Derwent Reservoir

As well as being unusual, Blanchland can claim to be one of the most attractive small villages not only in Northumberland but in the whole of England. The large square, based around the former large monastic courtyard, resembles an Italian piazza and to the north of it the arch of the former abbey gatehouse leads to another open space and groups of cottages. But this picturesque appearance was not always the case as in the early eighteenth century Blanchland was described as being in a poor and very dilapidated condition. It was the development of lead mining in the locality and consequent growth of population that led to the conversion of many of the derelict monastic buildings into the present cottages.

ⓧ ❶ Begin by crossing the road from the car park and turning left beside the White Monk Tearoom. At a public footpath sign, bear right along an enclosed uphill track which soon narrows to a path, curving left and continuing through woodland to a footpath post and junction of paths.

Keep ahead to emerge onto a grassy track, bear left along it and when you see a waymarked post on the right, head up to it and turn sharply right onto a path. The path continues gently uphill and gradually curves left to a ladder stile on the edge of the trees. Climb it, keep ahead to the brow of the hill, making for the next waymarked post, and continue across the hilltop to a kissing gate by a fence corner. Go through, keep ahead beside the fence – later a wall – on the left and climb a stile in the field corner. Ahead are grand views over the Derwent Reservoir.

ⓘ Derwent Reservoir, built in 1967, is the second largest reservoir in north east England and since its construction it has become a popular venue for sailing, fishing, bird watching, cycling and walking. Unlike some reservoirs which suffer from having an artificial appearance, its curved edges are more reminiscent of a natural lake.

ⓧ Continue along the left edge of a young plantation and after climbing a stile, keep ahead towards farm buildings. At a footpath sign, descend steps onto a road, turn left and follow the road for just over 800m (0.5 miles) to a public footpath sign to Acton. ❷ Turn right through a gate and walk diagonally downhill across a field to a stile in the bottom corner. Climb it, continue along a grassy path above a steep-sided valley, go through a gate and head down a steep embankment to a track. Keep along it towards Acton Farm, climb a stile, keep ahead and turn right through a kissing gate.

The River Derwent near Blanchland

Turn left onto a permissive path by a wall on the left that passes in front of the farmhouse and go through another kissing gate. Turn right, head gently downhill along a straight track and go through a gate onto a road. Turn right and follow the road to the bridge over the River Derwent. Do not cross it but turn right, at a public footpath sign to Blanchland, onto a wooded riverside path. ❸

Follow this delightful path back to Blanchland, a distance of about 2.4 km (1.5 miles). Descend steps to

cross a footbridge, keep ahead, climbing several stiles,
but at one point the path briefly turns right away from
the river because of riverbank erosion. Climb a stile, head
uphill by a wire fence on the left, follow the fence to the
left, climb two more stiles in quick succession and bear
left to regain the original riverside path. Continue by the
river to the bridge at Blanchland and the path bends right
in front of it into the village square. Keep ahead under
the arch of the former abbey gateway to return to the
start.

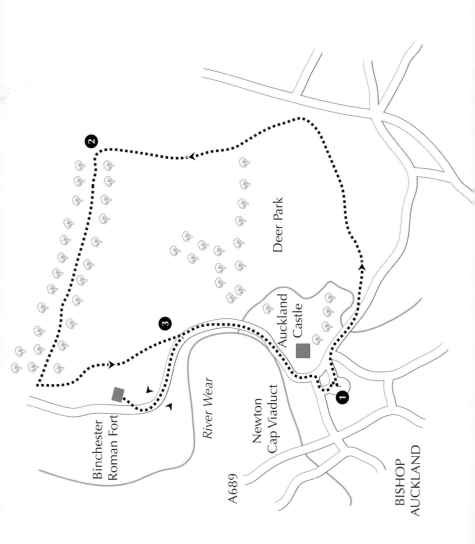

Deer Park

Auckland
Castle

River Wear

Newton
Cap Viaduct

A689

Binchester
Roman Fort

BISHOP
AUCKLAND

WALK 17

Bishop Auckland and Binchester Roman Fort

LENGTH:	8 km (5 miles)
TIME:	2.5 hours
TERRAIN:	Field and woodland paths and a middle section along a disused railway track
START/PARKING:	Bishop Auckland, Market Place, GR NZ212302. Pay car parks at Bishop Auckland
BUS/TRAIN:	Buses from Darlington, Durham and Barnard Castle; trains from Darlington and Durham
REFRESHMENTS:	Pubs and cafes at Bishop Auckland
MAP:	O.S. Explorer 305 – Bishop Auckland

The first part of the walk is beside the boundary wall of Auckland Deer Park. The route continues along a disused railway track and this is followed by a 2 km (1.25 miles) stretch through the delightful Belburn Wood. The final leg is along a quiet lane. There are fine views over the Wear valley and you have the opportunity to visit a Roman fort and the castle and deer park of the bishops of Durham.

Auckland Castle, palace of the bishops of Durham

ⓘ The large Market Place in Bishop Auckland is dominated by the handsome Victorian town hall, built in 1861. Leading off from the eastern end of it is the gatehouse of Auckland Castle, the official residence of the Bishops of Durham. It was originally built in the twelfth century as a hunting lodge for the powerful prince bishops but has been much restored and altered over the centuries. Pride of place goes to the magnificent chapel, converted in the seventeenth century from a medieval banqueting hall. Tel: 01388 601627

A walk through the Bishops Park, open to the public and part of the large deer park which once surrounded the castle, is well worthwhile. In it is the unusual Deer Shelter, a castellated and arcaded grassy quadrangle built in 1760.

❶ With the town hall and St Anne's church on your left, walk through the Market Place towards the gatehouse of Auckland Castle and Deer Park. Follow the road to the right and bear left at a junction, in the Spennymoor and Durham direction, heading down into a dip and up again.

Look out for a public footpath sign where you turn left up steps, climb a stile and keep ahead to climb another

Newton Cap Viaduct spans the River Wear at Bishop Auckland

one. The route now continues along the left edge of a
succession of fields and over a series of stiles beside the
boundary wall of the deer park – and later a golf course
– on the left. The last stile in the series brings you to a
T-junction where you turn left along a straight track, a
former railway line.

Pass under two bridges in quick succession, and later
under a third one. Just before crossing a bridge, turn left
to descend a flight of steps. ❷ Turn right over a stile and
now comes a most attractive part of the walk as you turn
left along a winding path through a long and narrow strip
of woodland (Belburn Wood), accompanied by the burn
at times which is forded twice. Eventually you climb a
stile on the far side of the wood and turn left.

Climb another stile, head gently uphill along the left

Remains of the Roman fort at Binchester

field edge and climb a stile in the top corner. Turn left
along the left edge of the next field, follow the edge to
the right, climb a stile, keep along the left field edge
and in the corner climb two stiles in quick succession.
Descend steps along the left inside edge of woodland and
continue along a path to a lane. ❸ Turn right and follow
the sign to the right up a tarmac drive to the entrance to
Binchester Roman Fort.

ℹ The Roman fort at Binchester was built in the first
century AD. It stands on Dere Street, an important road
that ran from York to the Scottish Borders, and its main
function was to protect the crossing point over the River
Wear. A short stretch of the original Dere Street survives
but the main feature is the Bath House attached to the
Commandant's House, one of the most impressive and
best preserved of its kind in the country. The fort covered
around 10 acres and could house up to 1000 soldiers. A
vicus or civilian settlement later grew up outside the walls
with shops, inns and a market place. Tel: 01388 663089

🚶 Retrace your steps along the lane and continue along it,
beside the River Wear, into Bishop Auckland. There are
views of Auckland Castle to the left and ahead is the
Newton Cap Viaduct.

ℹ Newton Cap Viaduct was built in the nineteenth century
to carry the railway line from Bishop Auckland to Durham
over the Wear valley. After the line closed, the viaduct
became ruined and was within a whisker of being
demolished but its conversion to a road bridge – it now
carries the A689 across the Wear – gave it a new lease of
life.

🚶 Follow the lane around a left bend and head uphill to
return to the Market Place.

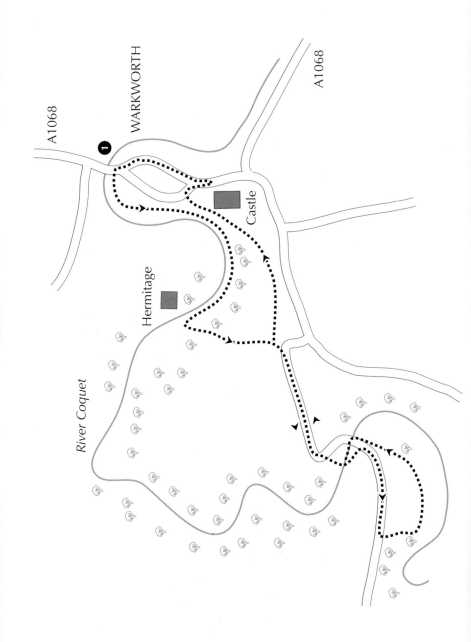

A1068

WARKWORTH

A1068

Castle

Hermitage

River Coquet

WALK 18

Warkworth Castle and Hermitage

LENGTH:	7.2 km (4.5 miles). There is a shorter walk of 4 km (2.5 miles)
TIME:	2 hours
TERRAIN:	Mainly wooded riverside paths and short stretches of quiet road walking, a few gentle climbs
START/PARKING:	Warkworth, by the fortified bridge over the River Coquet at the bottom (northern) end of the village, GR NU248063. Parking at Warkworth
BUS/TRAIN:	Buses from Newcastle, Morpeth and Alnwick
REFRESHMENTS:	Pubs and cafes at Warkworth
MAP:	O.S. Explorer 332 – Alnwick & Amble

Both the opening and closing stretches of the route are by the River Coquet and a large proportion of the walk is along wooded and secluded paths beside the meandering river, from which there are a series of superb views of Warkworth Castle. The castle is obviously the dominant but not the only historic feature; there is also the fortified bridge, Norman church and rare hermitage. The walk does a rough figure of eight to the south of the town and there is a shorter alternative that omits the second loop.

Fortified bridge over the River Coquet at Warkworth

Warkworth Castle above the River Coquet

In the Middle Ages many towns in Britain had fortified bridges but the one over the River Coquet at Warkworth is one of the few that have survived. It was built in the fourteenth century and the tower had a lock-up cell.

❶ Facing the bridge, take the tarmac riverside path to the left of it, signposted Monks Walk, passing Warkworth's twelfth-century church on the left. Keep ahead along a road by a parking area and continue along a tree-lined riverside path, at a public footpath sign Mill Wood and Howlet Hall, following it around a right bend. At this point look back for a superb view of Warkworth Castle. After going through a kissing gate, walk across a meadow to a public footpath sign opposite Warkworth Hermitage.

The extensive remains of Warkworth Castle and opposite, wooded banks of the River Coquet near Warkworth

ⓘ The Hermitage comprises living quarters and a chapel cut from the rock of the wooded riverbank and is thought to date from the early fourteenth century. It is only accessible in the summer by rowing boat. For details of opening times check at the castle. Tel: 01665 711423

⚐ **Turn sharp left along a track away from the river, heading uphill to a kissing gate. Go through, keep ahead to a T-junction and bear left along a tarmac drive to reach a road at a bend. ❷**

 If doing the short walk, turn left just before the road at a public footpath sign and follow the route directions from where ❷ appears in the text again.

For the full walk, turn right along the road (Watershaugh Road) and keep ahead downhill along a lane. After a left bend, look out for a narrow tarmac path on the right which heads downhill to cross a footbridge over the Coquet. On the other side, turn left onto a riverside path – be careful here as the path slopes in places and is uneven – to emerge onto the lane again. Turn right, follow the lane around a right bend, head uphill and at a public bridleway sign, turn left through a gate. ❸

Walk gently downhill along the left edge of woodland and look out for a public bridleway sign where you turn left through a gate. Keep along the top left edge of a field – the river is below you across the field – and bear left to a gate. Go through, continue along an enclosed track to rejoin the lane you were previously on and from here retrace your steps to ❷.

Where the road bends right, keep ahead, at a public footpath sign to Warkworth Castle, along a right field edge, here joining the shorter walk. The path bears left to a gate. Go through, continue in the same direction diagonally across the next two fields and in the third field, take the path along its left edge towards the castle.

❶ The splendid, well-preserved and extensive remains of Warkworth Castle occupy the highest point at the south end of the village and stand within a loop of the River Coquet. The present castle was begun in the thirteenth century and the impressive gatehouse and many of the towers and much of the outer walls date from that period. In the early fourteenth century the castle passed to the powerful Percy family, earls and later dukes of Northumberland, and they carried out a series of major additions and alterations to strengthen the castle against Scottish attacks. Their most outstanding contribution was the magnificent keep, almost a castle in itself, built in the shape of a Greek cross and in an excellent state of preservation.

The warlike and troublesome Percys spent almost as much time rebelling against the monarch as keeping the Scots at bay and several times they forfeited the castle only to regain it at a later date. After the 7th Earl of Northumberland played a leading role in the Rising of the North – an unsuccessful rebellion against Elizabeth I for which he was executed in 1572 – the castle was abandoned and fell into decay. There was a later minor restoration but the Percys preferred to concentrate on their main residence at nearby Alnwick, leaving Warkworth as a ruin but more complete than most with a fine range of buildings to explore. Tel: 01665 711423

🚶 **In the field corner, descend steps and continue below the castle walls to emerge onto a road at the top of Castle Street. ❹ Turn right, follow the road around a right bend and when you see steps on the left, descend them and turn left along a lower road (Wellfield). The road curves first right and then left and continues by the river to the start.**

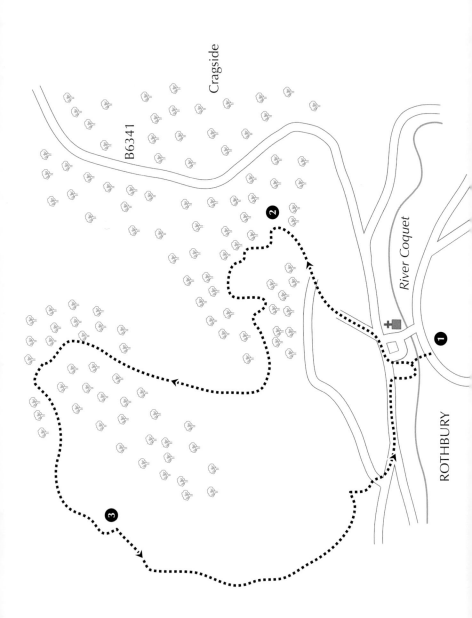

Cragside

B6341

River Coquet

ROTHBURY

WALK 19

Above Rothbury

LENGTH:	8.9 km (5.5 miles)
TIME:	3 hours
TERRAIN:	Clear paths through woodland and across moorland, steady climb just after the start
START/PARKING:	Rothbury, Cowhaugh car park on the south side of the River Coquet, GR NU057015
BUS/TRAIN:	Buses from Newcastle, Morpeth and Alnwick
REFRESHMENTS:	Pubs and cafes at Rothbury
MAP:	Explorer 332 – Alnwick & Amble

After an initial climb through woodland, the route continues through more woods and across moorland above Rothbury before descending back into the town. From the higher points you enjoy a series of magnificent and wide ranging views over Coquetdale and the Simonside Hills and across open country to the line of the Cheviots. The walk makes use of some of the carriage drives laid out in the nineteenth century by Lord Armstrong on his nearby Cragside Estate. The fascinating house and grand parkland of Cragside, about 2.4 km (1.5 miles) from Rothbury, is well worth a visit at the end of the walk.

Looking over the Coquet Valley to the Simonside Hills from above Rothbury

🚶 ❶ **Cross the footbridge over the River Coquet and walk along an enclosed tarmac path and then a lane into Rothbury town centre.**

ℹ This attractive little town, situated in the heart of Coquetdale and surrounded by glorious countryside, is an excellent walking centre. Just off the main street is the church, on an ancient site but mostly rebuilt in the middle of the nineteenth century. In the lower part of the graveyard across the road are the family graves of some of the Armstrongs, including Lord Armstrong (1810–1900), one of the most prominent Victorian inventors and industrialists and builder of Cragside House.

🚶 **Turn right down High Street and turn left beside the Queens Head into Brewery Lane. The lane bears right uphill and curves first left and then right. Look out for where you turn left along a track between bungalows to a public footpath sign to Alnwick Road and a kissing gate. Go through, head uphill along an enclosed path which bears right across a field to another kissing gate,** go through that one and continue uphill. Go through a kissing gate and up steps to a road, turn right and where the road ends, keep ahead along a track by the right edge of woodland.

Just beyond the corner of the wood, turn left up steps and go through a gate. Bear slightly right, head uphill across a field and go through kissing gate at the top. ❷ Do not go through the next kissing gate immediately ahead but turn left along a track, one of the Cragside carriage drives.

ⓘ The thick woodlands over to the right are part of the Cragside Estate. The grand Victorian house at Cragside, situated high up amidst acres of hills, woods and lakes, was the creation of William Armstrong – later Lord Armstrong – one of the great figures of the Victorian age. The house, designed by Norman Shaw, was the most technologically advanced of the time and reflects Armstrong's engineering ingenuity and interests. It was the first house to use hydro-electricity, with lighting and lifts all run on hydraulic power, the water coming from the man made lakes in the grounds. Armstrong was also a man of wide artistic tastes and interests and the house possesses a fine collection of

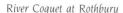

River Coquet at Rothbury

The grave of Lord Armstrong, Tyneside industrialist and builder of Cragside, in the churchyard at Rothbury Church

Victorian paintings and furniture. Cragside is surrounded by a variety of formal gardens and many of the trees in the extensive wooded parkland were imported from around the world.

In the nineteenth century the estate was bigger than now. The house, gardens and parkland that are now owned and maintained by the National Trust lie just to the east of the B6341 but this area of land on the other side of the road is still owned by the Armstrong family. The carriage drives were used by Lord Armstrong and his family and friends for outings from Cragside and provide superb views over the surrounding countryside. Tel: 01669 620333

Head gently uphill through beautiful beech woodland and at a fork take the right hand upper track which continues winding through the wood for about 1.2 km (0.75 miles) before descending to a kissing gate on the edge of the trees. Ahead is open moorland.

After going through the kissing gate, keep ahead to a fingerpost at a crossways and turn right onto a path that heads across the moor. On the far side cross a footbridge to re-enter woodland, go through a gate and a few yards ahead, bear right onto a track. Follow it to a T-junction and turn left along a track signposted 'Public Road to Snitter'. Head uphill to a crossways where you turn left through a gate, in the Thropton and Rothbury direction, and continue along a track which emerges into open moorland. The all round views from here are superb.

Look out for a crossways just before a right bend where you turn right ❸ off the main stony track and continue along a grassy path parallel to your previous track, later joining and keeping by a wall on the right. Follow this undulating path – later a track – to a gate. Go through and the track bends right downhill, turns left and continues down to a lane. Turn right and at a T-junction, turn left along a road which descends into Rothbury.

Bear left on joining a main road and continue down into the town centre. Turn right along Well Strand which leads to the river, turn left beside it and turn right over the footbridge to return to the car park.

Rothbury Church

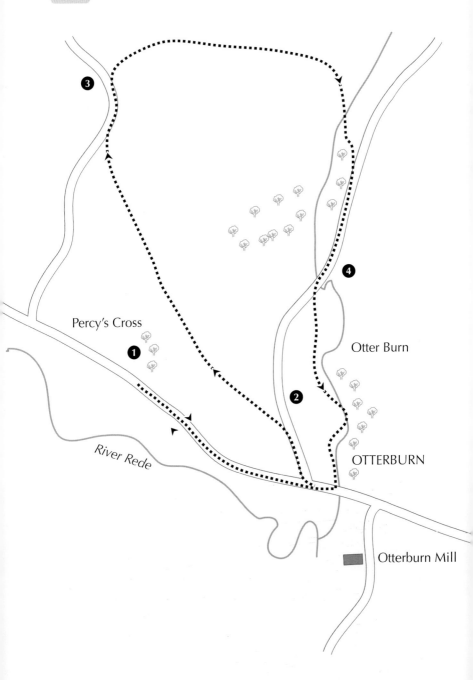

Percy's Cross

River Rede

Otter Burn

OTTERBURN

Otterburn Mill

WALK 20

Battle of Otterburn

LENGTH:	8.9 km (5.5 miles)
TIME:	3 hours
TERRAIN:	Mainly moorland tracks and riverside path, some road walking
START/PARKING:	Otterburn Battle Site, on A696 about 1.2 km (0.75 miles) to the west of Otterburn village, GR NY876935
BUS/TRAIN:	Buses from Newcastle
REFRESHMENTS:	Pub and café at Otterburn, café at Otterburn Mill about 183m (200 yards) to the south of the village
MAP:	O.S. Explorer OL42 – Kielder Water & Forest

The walk starts at an information site for the battle and takes you across the heart of the battlefield, from where there are extensive views over the empty landscape of Redesdale. You continue across open moorland before descending into the valley of the Otter Burn and a pleasant stretch beside the wooded banks of the burn leads into the village. The final leg is along the road.

Note that part of the route crosses a Military Firing Range which you must not enter when red flags or lights are displayed or the barriers are closed. Before starting out it is advisable to phone 01830 520569 or 0191 239 4261 for information on this.

1 Apart from Bannockburn and Flodden, the battle of
Otterburn is probably one of the best known of the many
border conflicts between England and Scotland. Although
there is some dispute as to the precise date, it is generally
thought to have taken place on 19 August 1388.

It was fought between the Percy (English) and Douglas
(Scottish) families, two of the most famous of the rival
border families with a longstanding feud. In 1388 James
Earl of Douglas led a raiding party into northern England,
burning and pillaging Durham, but was stopped during
a skirmish just outside Newcastle by Henry Percy
– nicknamed Hotspur – and his brother Ralph. It is alleged

Information board on the site of the Battle of Otterburn

Overlooking Redesdale and the battlefield of Otterburn

that during this skirmish Douglas captured Hotspur's lance pennon – his personal flag – and taunted him to recover it, an insult and challenge that the Percies could not ignore.

On his return to Scotland, with the Percy brothers in hot pursuit, Douglas set up camp in Redesdale just to the west of Otterburn and waited to do battle with them. The English army reached there on the evening of 19 August and surprisingly Hotspur decided on an immediate battle rather than wait for the morning. This proved to be a disastrous decision: his men were tired after a long march and in a night battle, the English archers, whose longbow attacks were frequently the main reason for victories over the Scots, would be largely ineffective.

Furthermore Hotspur's strategy of a two-pronged assault on Douglas failed. He sent Sir Thomas Umfraville on a march to the north and east of the Scottish army to outflank them and attack from the rear while he and his main body of troops launched a frontal attack. But the Scots, superbly led by Douglas, held the English, drove them back and scattered them. During the fierce fighting both Hotspur and his brother Ralph were captured but the Scottish victory was somewhat soured by the death of Douglas. The battle was virtually over before Umfraville was able to play a part in it and it was he who led the defeated English army away. The Scots returned home and the Percy brothers were later released.

⊛ ❶ **There are two information boards in the car park, one of which overlooks the battlefield across which you will shortly walk, plus the Percy Cross, erected in 1777 as a monument to the Percy brothers. Begin by turning left along the road into Otterburn – there is a footpath all the way – and take the first road on the left, signposted to Otterburn Hall. At a public bridleway sign, turn left along a track, ❷ go through a gate and continue between farm buildings.**

Go through a gate and walk along the left edge of a field, by a wall on the left. After the next gate, keep by a wall on the right, go through another gate and continue in the same direction across uneven ground, making for a gate and waymarked post.

❶ This is the heart of the battlefield and the scene of some of the fiercest fighting. Looking over the valley, the main English army was to the left near the village and the Scots occupied the higher ground ahead.

(図) Go through the gate and head gently uphill – at this stage there is no visible path – passing to the right of a small group of widely spaced trees and looking out for a footpath post. At the post turn right onto an uphill narrow lane and about 91m (100 yards) beyond a left bend, turn right, ❸ at a public bridleway sign, along a faint path across open moorland. Walk past a circular sheep pen and continue on to a waymarked gate.

At this point there are prominent danger notices warning you that the area ahead is a Military Firing Range and you must not enter when there are red lights or flags displayed or when the barriers are closed.

After going through the gate, head gradually downhill, later keeping parallel to a fence on the right, and make for a public bridleway sign to Hopefoot Cottages at the bottom where you go through a gate onto a tarmac track. Turn right, at the next bridleway sign turn left along a track and at a fingerpost, turn right along a grassy track which keeps above the Otter Burn on the left. Descend to cross a footbridge over the burn, head uphill and go through a gate into a small conifer wood. Keep ahead, turn left at a waymarked post, go through a gate to leave the trees and turn right along a road.

After about 800m (0.5 miles), turn left through a kissing gate, ❹ at a public footpath sign to Otterburn, and walk diagonally across a field, later keeping by a fence on the right to a gate. Go through, bear right along a path above the burn, head down to cross a footbridge and go through another gate. Continue along an undulating path – sometimes above and sometimes beside the burn – finally emerging onto a tarmac track by houses.

Keep ahead to emerge onto the main road in Otterburn opposite the Percy Arms. To return to the start turn right and follow the road for 1.2 km (0.75 mile) – soon picking up the outward route.

If you wish to visit Otterburn Mill, turn left, passing the Otterburn Tower Hotel, on the site of a Norman castle, and turn right along the B6320.

ⓘ A visit to Otterburn Mill, a former woollen mill, is worth the short detour. It retains some of the original mill machinery and has a gift shop, café and pleasant riverside garden.

The Percy Cross commemorates the Battle of Otterburn

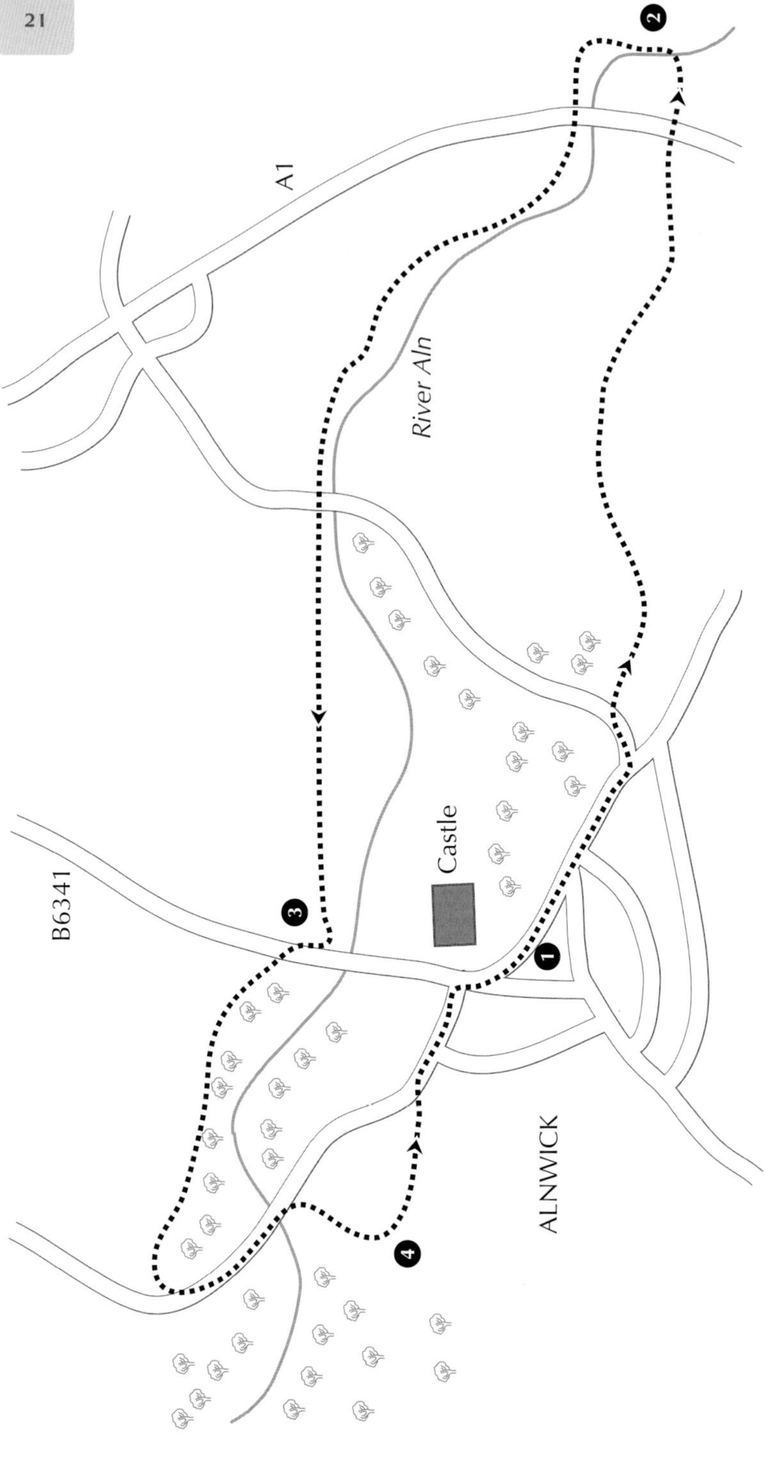

A1

River Aln

B6341

Castle

ALNWICK

2

3

1

4

WALK 21

Alnwick and the River Aln

LENGTH:	8 km (5 miles)
TIME:	2.5 hours
TERRAIN:	Flat and easy walking, much of it along riverside paths
START/PARKING:	Alnwick, Market Place, GR NU187134. Pay car parks at Alnwick
BUS/TRAIN:	Buses from Newcastle, Morpeth, Berwick upon Tweed and nearby towns
REFRESHMENTS:	Pubs and cafes at Alnwick and several cafes at Alnwick Castle and Garden
MAP:	Explorer 332 – Alnwick & Amble

The highlight of this walk in the countryside around Alnwick is the stroll along the riverside path beside the Aln, especially the stretch across meadows from where you enjoy a succession of magnificent views of Alnwick Castle on the opposite bank. Elsewhere there is pleasant woodland and the various attractions of Alnwick itself, a most appealing town.

❶ From the Market Place, start by walking eastwards along Bondgate Within towards the Hotspur Gate. Beyond the gate the road continues as Bondgate Without and the first road on the left leads to the entrance to Alnwick Castle and the Alnwick Garden.

ⓘ In the Middle Ages Alnwick was a walled town but the
fifteenth-century Bondgate (sometimes called the Hotspur
Gate after one of the most famous members of the Percy
family) is all that remains of its medieval defences. It was
the main entrance into the town.

The great castle however survives intact and is one
of a handful of castles in England that has made the
transition from medieval fortress to palatial residence. The
first castle on the site was built soon after the Norman

*Opposite: In the Middle Ages Bondgate was the main entrance into Alnwick
Rolling countryside near Alnwick*

Conquest. In 1309 it was purchased from the bishop of
Durham by Henry Percy and has been the chief residence
of the powerful Percy family – later earls and dukes of
Northumberland – ever since.

As a border fortress, Alnwick Castle was frequently
the target of Scottish attacks and was strengthened and
rebuilt at regular intervals but by the late seventeenth
century it had fallen into a poor state. Internal alterations
were carried out by Adam in the eighteenth century but
the present appearance of the castle is largely the result
of a comprehensive restoration by Salvin in the nineteenth
century. The lavish and spacious state rooms include the
drawing room, library and dining room and contain a fine

Alnwick Castle

collection of paintings, furnishings and porcelain amassed by the Percys. Visitors also see the nineteenth-century Gothic chapel. The grounds surrounding the castle were landscaped in the eighteenth century by Capability Brown. Tel: 01665 510777

A recent additional attraction adjacent to the castle is the Alnwick Garden, a contemporary formal garden with a grand cascade and what claims to be the world's largest tree house. Its interesting design and relaxing atmosphere make it well worth a visit. Tel: 01665 511350

Ⓧ **Continue along Bondgate Without and turn left along the B1340, signposted to Bamburgh. Where the road bends left, turn right along a walled tarmac track which narrows to become an enclosed path. Cross a road, keep ahead, go through a kissing gate and continue along the right edge of a field. After the next kissing gate, walk along a left field edge and go through a gate onto a lane at a bend.**

Bear left along an enclosed track which passes under the A1, go through another kissing gate and keep ahead to cross a footbridge over the River Aln. At a footpath post a short distance ahead, turn left ❷ onto a riverside path which follows the river around a left bend. For the next 2.4 km (1.5 miles) the route keeps by the Aln.

Go through a gate, pass under the A1 again, go through several more gates and after following a winding path through woodland you head up to a road to the right of a bridge. Cross over and at a public footpath sign to Lion Bridge, go through a kissing gate and take the path ahead. It is on this stretch of the walk across The Pastures, part of the landscaped parkland adjoining Alnwick Castle, that you enjoy a series of magnificent views of the castle on the opposite bank of the river. The river meanders off to the left but the route continues in a fairly straight line across the meadows, rejoining the river

Alnwick Castle

nears the far end where you go through a kissing gate to emerge onto a road to the right of the Lion Bridge. ❸

Turn right uphill and at a public footpath sign, turn left to go through a kissing gate and continue alongside a wall bordering woodland on the left. After the next kissing gate, walk along an enclosed path – later it becomes first a gravel track and then a concrete drive – to reach a road. Turn left downhill, cross a bridge over the river and at public footpath and bridleway signs, turn right through a gate. Walk along an enclosed path which curves slightly left to a gate. Go through, head uphill across a field and at the top go through a kissing gate onto a tarmac drive. ❹

To the right is the entrance to Hulne Park, an extensive former deer park also belonging to the dukes of Northumberland. It houses two monastic ruins, the scanty remains of Alnwick Abbey and the more substantial ruins of Hulne Priory.

Turn left and on joining a road (Bailiffgate), keep along it back into the town. At a T-junction in front of the castle gatehouse, turn right and the road bends left to return to the start.

Alnwick Castle

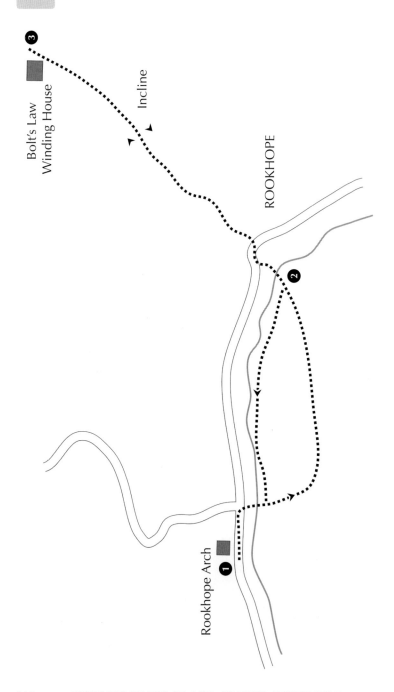

Bolt's Law
Winding House

Incline

ROOKHOPE

Rookhope Arch

WALK 22

Rookhope and Relics of the Lead Mining Industry

LENGTH:	7.2 km (4.5 miles)
TIME:	2 hours
TERRAIN:	Mostly along clear paths and tracks with two steady climbs
START/PARKING:	Rookhope Arch, about 1.6 km (1 mile) west of Rookhope village on the minor road that leads off to the north from the A689 at Eastgate 4 km (2.5 miles) to the west of Stanhope, GR NY924430
BUS/TRAIN:	Buses from Stanhope
REFRESHMENTS:	Pub at Rookhope
MAP:	Explorer 307 – Consett & Derwent Reservoir

This is a walk in the remote valley of Rookhope Burn, one of many former lead mining areas scattered throughout the dales of the North Pennines. The first part takes you above the south side of the dale before dropping into the village of Rookhope. Next comes a 'there and back' walk up a former railway incline to the remains of Bolt's Law Winding House. The last stretch is a relaxing stroll by the burn. The many fine views over the dale are enhanced by the forlorn and atmospheric remains of the lead mining industry.

ⓘ The earliest reference to lead mining in Weardale and its adjacent valleys is in the twelfth century but it may have been carried out since Roman times. The industry expanded rapidly during the eighteenth century and reached its peak around the middle of the nineteenth century when these now quiet and isolated dales, like the area around Rookhope, were busy and noisy centres of industrial activity with small lead, iron and other mineral workings scattered throughout them, linked by railways. The decline of this mining activity was even more rapid, largely the result of competition from much larger mines in America and Australia, and few lead mines survived much beyond World War I.

Rookhope Arch is all that remains of a group of buildings that comprised Lintzgarth Smelt Mill. The mill smelted lead ore from the various mines along the valley into pigs or bars of lead. There were originally six arches carrying a 3.2 km (2 mile) long horizontal stone flue over Rookhope Burn which took poisonous gases from the mines to be discharged on the moors. The mill closed down in 1923.

❶ Turn left along the road and at a Lead Mining Trail public footpath sign opposite the road to Blanchland, turn right over a stile. Cross a footbridge over Rookhope Burn, head up over uneven ground, passing to the right of a house, curve left around the end of the house and turn right along a track. After going through a gate, turn left onto an enclosed track, at a Mineral Valleys Way sign, and head uphill, curving gradually left along the side of the valley.

At a fork take the left hand lower track and keep ahead, going through two gates. The track descends slightly and curves left to pass in front of a white house. Before reaching the next house, turn left off the track and look out for a gate in the wall on the right. Go

Rookhope Arch, isolated relic of the Durham lead mining industry

through and head gently downhill across three fields,
negotiating two stone stiles and a gate, to reach farm
buildings. Keep ahead in front of the buildings, climb
a waymarked stile and continue downhill towards
Rookhope, descending steeply to another stile. After
climbing it, keep ahead, crossing first a track and then a
bridge over the burn, ❷ and continue into the village.

❶ The village of Rookhope was originally two small
agricultural settlements that merged into one when they
expanded with the development of lead mining and
smelting in the vicinity. At one time it was roughly twice its

Overlooking Rookhope

present size and like many of the other lead mining villages in Weardale, it was a thriving community with shops, schools, chapels, pubs and sports clubs. Now the mines, smelting works and railways have all gone, the village has shrunk and largely reverted to its earlier tranquillity.

🚶 **Turn right along a road, passing the Rookhope Inn, and where the road bends right, keep ahead along a track, signposted Rookhope Trails Walk 4. For the next 1.6 km (1 mile) you head steadily uphill along a track, formerly** a railway incline. At a fork continue along the right hand uphill track, at the next fork take the left hand track, go through a gate and continue up to the atmospheric remains of Bolt's Law Winding House and Engine Shed at the top of the incline. ❸

 The surviving industrial buildings at the top of the Bolt's Law Incline housed the standing engine and winding gear

Top of the Bolt's Law Incline

Bolt's Law Winding House and Engine Shed

that controlled the movement of trucks up and down the incline. The railway was constructed in the middle of the nineteenth century by the Weardale Iron Company and the trucks, hauled by wire ropes, carried coal to Rookhope for the smelt mill and transported lead and iron ore from the mines and limestone from the local quarries across the moors to the blast furnaces around Tow Law and to the banks of the River Tyne.

🚶 **Retrace your steps down into the village and over Rookhope Burn ❷ and at a footpath sign Rookhope**

Trails Walk 2 just ahead, turn right along a track beside the burn. Go through a gate, keep ahead and just before reaching houses, bear slightly left up to a gate. After going through it, you regain the track and soon Rookhope Arch comes into view. Go through another gate, keep ahead, climb a stile and turn right over a footbridge. Here you rejoin the outward route and retrace your steps the short distance to the start.

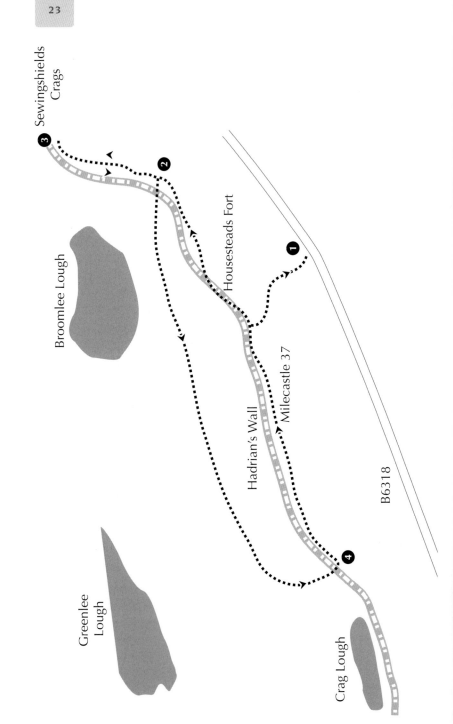

Sewingshields
Crags

③

②

Broomlee Lough

Housesteads Fort

①

Hadrian's Wall

Milecastle 37

B6318

Greenlee Lough

④

Crag Lough

WALK 23

Hadrian's Wall near Housesteads

LENGTH:	9.7 km (6 miles). There is a shorter walk of 8 km (5 miles) which omits the detour to Sewingshields Crags
TIME:	3 hours
TERRAIN:	Most of the walk is an up and down route – strenuous in places – beside Hadrian's Wall; the rest is across flat but rough grassland which could be boggy after rainy weather
START/PARKING:	National Trust pay car park at Housesteads Roman Fort, on B3618 (Military Road), GR NY794684
BUS/TRAIN:	Housesteads is served by the Hadrian's Wall Bus, appropriately numbered AD122, which runs the whole length of the wall between Wallsend and Bowness-on-Solway and operates on Sundays and Bank Holidays between Easter and the end of October and daily between the end of May and end of September
REFRESHMENTS:	Kiosk serving drinks and snacks by the information centre
MAP:	O.S. Explorer OL43 – Hadrian's Wall

The walk takes you along what is arguably the finest, best-preserved and most spectacular stretch of Hadrian's Wall and provides a series of extensive and magnificent views. It gives you the opportunity to visit the most complete of the several forts along the wall, passes a milecastle and enables you to appreciate the strength and sheer engineering brilliance of the wall from the perspective both of the soldiers who manned it and those to the north who might aspire to attack it.

Housesteads, the most complete Roman fort on Hadrian's Wall

*The Roman fort and its associated civilian settlement lie amid
spectacular countryside, just south of the wall*

❶ **Start by going under the arch by the entrance to
the information centre and curving left to go through a
kissing gate. Continue up to the fort and where the path
bends left to the museum, keep ahead uphill across grass
beside the west wall of the fort to a gate.**

ⓘ The construction of a wall across northern England from
the Tyne to the Solway was ordered by the Emperor
Hadrian around AD 122 in order to make this part of his
empire more secure. It is approximately 117.5 km (73 miles)
long and had a variety of functions, both military and
non-military. It clearly marked the northern border of the
Roman province of Britain, was a base for dealing with
attacks from the north and possible rebellions by the tribes

Knag Burn Gateway, an official crossing point on Hadrian's Wall

to the south within the empire, and it made it possible to regulate and define the crossing points on the frontier.

It formed part of what was a huge military complex. As well as the wall itself, there were 17 forts built along its length, between them were a series of milecastles or mini-forts, built at intervals of approximately a mile, and between the milecastles were turrets or look-out posts. The wall was about 4.6m (15 feet) high and between 2.4 and 3 metres (8 to 10 feet) wide. On its north side it was protected by a V-shaped ditch, except where steep cliffs made this extra defence unnecessary, and to the south was a wide, flat-bottomed ditch called the vallum. The purpose of this has been a matter of controversy but it may have marked the boundary between the military zone around the wall and the civilian zone to the south. In addition a road, the Military Way, ran between the wall and the vallum linking the wall forts and a few miles to the south another road, the Stanegate, connected a series of back-up forts.

Despite all this military sophistication, the wall was overrun on a number of occasions and was continually being modernised and partially rebuilt. During the second century it was briefly abandoned when the Romans decided to advance further north and establish a new frontier between the Clyde and Forth, the Antonine Wall. They later withdrew back to Hadrian's Wall and reinstated it as their permanent frontier. It was finally abandoned in the early fifth century when the Romans withdrew all their forces from Britain.

Housesteads is the best-preserved and most complete of the wall forts. Like most of the forts throughout the Roman Empire it has a playing card shape and you can wander around the extensive remains of the headquarters building (the administrative centre of the fort), commandant's house, barracks, granaries and latrines. Some of the foundations of the vicus, the civilian settlement that grew up just outside the walls of the fort, can also be seen. Tel: 01434 344363

Go through the gate, turn right and immediately descend a flight of steps. Keep beside the wall, which here forms the north wall of the fort, and at the north east corner of the fort, the wall bends left and descends to Knag Burn Gateway where you turn right through a kissing gate.

Knag Burn Gateway is a rare example of a gate in Hadrian's Wall that is not at a fort or milecastle. It was built in the fourth century probably to provide an alternative

Classsic view of Hadrian's Wall and opposite, looking back to Housesteads from Knag Burn

crossing place for the heavy traffic wanting to pass through the wall at Housesteads.

🚶 **Turn left in the Sewingshields direction – now with the wall on the left – head up to climb a stone stile and continue through a group of trees. Climb a ladder stile at the far end of the trees and continue along a switchback route beside the wall until you reach a ladder stile on the left. ❷**

For the shorter route turn left over this stile but for the full walk – eminently worthwhile – keep ahead for another 800m (0.5 mile), climbing up to the trig point on Sewingshields Crags. ❸

❶ From this magnificent vantage point, 325m (1066 feet) high and the main reason for the detour, the views extend for miles across open and lonely country from the South Tyne valley to the edge of the vast Border Forests. Westwards the view is dominated by the austere and chilly looking waters of Broomlee Lough.

Retrace your steps downhill to the ladder stile, ❷ turn right over it and follow a faint path in a straight line across rough grass towards a group of conifers. Climb a stile, keep ahead through the trees, climb a stile on the far side and continue across the rough grassland. To the left are grand views of the wall stretching along cliff tops and rising and falling like a roller coaster, a formidable sight for any potential attackers.

Later the path passes between a conifer plantation on the left and the waters of Greenlee Lough on the right. Bear left on meeting another path and ahead is a great view of the wall perched on the top of the precipitous cliffs of Highshield Crags with Crag Lough below. Head towards a farm and keep to the left of the farm buildings to reach a stone stile.

After climbing it, turn left over a ladder stile ❹ to rejoin the Hadrian's Wall Path for the remainder of the route, a fairly strenuous up and down walk with several steep stretches. It is on this part of the walk that you enjoy the popular picture postcard views of the wall looking ahead to Cuddy's Crags, Housesteads and in the far distance your previous viewpoint of Sewingshields Crags. After about 1.6 km (1 mile) you reach Milecastle 37.

ⓘ Milecastle 37 is one of the best-preserved examples of the numerous mini-forts on the wall. It is a smaller version of Housesteads with neat rows of barracks and a gateway.

🚶 **From the milecastle a short walk through a small group of trees brings you back to Housesteads Fort. Turn right through the gate passed through previously and retrace your steps downhill to the start.**

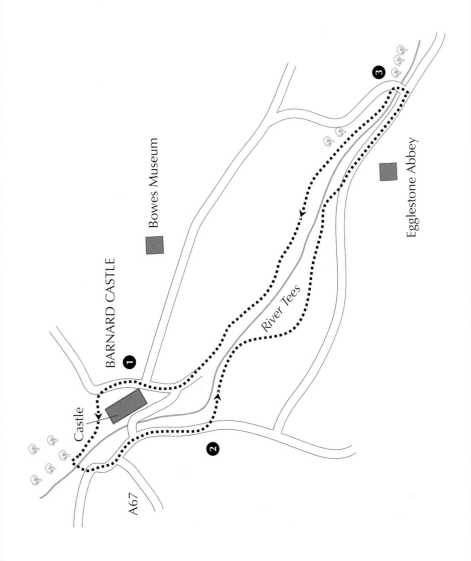

Bowes Museum

BARNARD CASTLE

Egglestone Abbey

River Tees

Castle

A67

WALK 24

Barnard Castle and Egglestone Abbey

LENGTH:	7.2 km (4.5 miles)
TIME:	2 hours
TERRAIN:	Undulating riverside and woodland paths
START/PARKING:	Barnard Castle, by the Market Cross, GR NY051163. Parking at Barnard Castle
BUS/TRAIN:	Buses from Darlington, Bishop Auckland and Richmond
REFRESHMENTS:	Pubs and cafes at Barnard Castle
MAP:	O.S. Explorer OL31 – North Pennines – Teesdale & Weardale

This superb short walk takes you along both banks of the River Tees downstream from Barnard Castle, mainly across meadows and through sloping woodland. It links two impressive medieval ruins, both of which are enhanced by their fine settings above the river.

❶ The fine old town of Barnard Castle gets its name from Bernard de Balliol who began the construction of the castle in the early twelfth century. The Balliols were a prominent family who owned much of the surrounding area. One member of the family, John, married into the Scottish aristocracy and his son – also named John – briefly

occupied the Scottish throne. Another Balliol founded the Oxford college that bears his name.

The castle, a most impressive sight when seen from below, sprawls over a large area crowning a ridge above the River Tees. Substantial sections of its walls and towers remain but the most prominent feature is the three-storied circular keep, the Balliol Tower, built in the thirteenth century. Following the decline of the Balliol family fortunes in the fourteenth century, the castle had various owners but was largely neglected by them. In 1569 it was besieged and captured by rebel forces during the 'Rising of the North' a Catholic rebellion against the establishment of the Protestant Church of England by Elizabeth I. After this event it continued to deteriorate and fell into ruin, a process hastened by the fact that one of its owners used it as a source of building material for one of his other residences. Tel: 01833 638212

❶ The walk starts in the town centre by the medieval church and eighteenth-century Market Cross. Dairy produce was sold at the latter, hence its alternative name Butter Cross. With your back to the church, turn right through Market Place and along Horse Market. At the corner of Horse Market and Galgate, turn left along a tarmac drive towards the castle and at a fork, take the right hand path, signposted Riverside Walk and Cotherstone.

Head downhill, bearing left and then turning right beside the River Tees and turn left to cross a footbridge over the river. From here there are grand views both upstream and downstream and arguably the finest view of the castle. Keep ahead to a road and turn left along the south side of the castle. Pass the bridge, continue along the road beside the river and at a public footpath

Opposite: Barnard Castle

River Tees downstream from Barnard Castle

sign where the river bends left, ❷ turn left onto a
narrow path beside it.

Keep ahead at a footbridge and at a fork, take the
left hand path, continuing by the Tees. The path bends
right, heads slightly uphill and the route continues to
the left along a tarmac drive through a caravan site. At
a footpath post turn right uphill, turn left and continue
gently uphill to emerge from the caravan site. Look out
for where you climb a waymarked stile on the left, head
across grass and pass through a hedge gap between
redundant gateposts.

ⓘ Over to the left a large building that looks like a French chateau can be seen on the horizon. This is the Bowes Museum, built in the late nineteenth century by John Bowes as a museum and art gallery. It houses a fine art collection and is well worth a visit. Tel: 01833 690606

⊛ The path continues along the left edge of several fields before bearing right through a squeezer stile onto a lane. Turn left downhill and continue below the ruins of Egglestone Abbey to Abbey Bridge.

The ruins of Egglestone Abbey above the Tees

ⓘ Egglestone Abbey occupies an idyllic position on a ridge overlooking the thickly-wooded banks of the Tees. The abbey belonged to the Premonstratensian order of canons and was founded round 1195. It was always among the smaller and poorer monastic houses and suffered during the Anglo-Scottish wars of the fourteenth century. At the time of its dissolution by Henry VIII and Thomas Cromwell in 1536, its income was calculated at only £37.

The remains date mainly from the thirteenth and fourteenth centuries, notably the east and west ends of the church and a few of the domestic buildings. Some of the surviving buildings around the cloister were converted into a Tudor house following the closure of the abbey.

Egglestone Abbey

Egglestone Abbey

Ⓧ Turn left over the bridge, immediately turn left again through a squeezer stile, ❸ at a public footpath sign, and walk along an undulating path through sloping woodland above the rocky, gushing waters of the Tees. After going through a kissing gate, continue across a series of riverside meadows, enjoying a succession of spectacular views of the abbey above the opposite bank. At one point bear slightly right away from the river to go through a gate and then continue as before across a meadow by the river.

Eventually you go through a gate and walk along an enclosed path which passes between farm buildings and then widens into a track. Go through a kissing gate, keep ahead towards houses and where the track ends, continue along a road to a T-junction. Turn right uphill to return to the start.

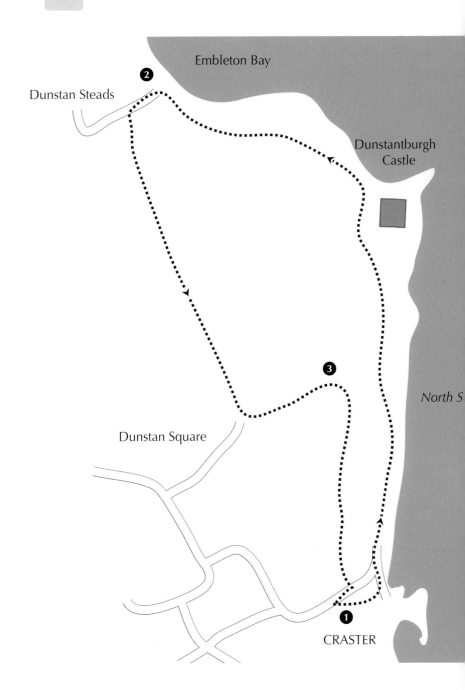

Embleton Bay

Dunstan Steads

Dunstantburgh
Castle

North S

Dunstan Square

CRASTER

WALK 25

Craster and Dunstantburgh Castle

LENGTH:	8 km (5 miles)
TIME:	2.5 hours
TERRAIN:	Easy walking across low cliffs and along tracks and field paths
START/PARKING:	Pay car park at Craster, GR NU256198
BUS/TRAIN:	Buses from Alnwick and Bamburgh
REFRESHMENTS:	Pub and restaurant/coffee shop at Craster
MAP:	O.S. Explorer 332 – Alnwick & Amble

Immediately on leaving the harbour at Craster, there are stunning views ahead of the gaunt ruins of Dunstantburgh Castle, situated on a rocky cliff above the North Sea. Beyond the castle, the route continues by Embleton Bay before turning inland for the return half of the walk. The castle continues in sight as you head up over the whinstone ridge of The Heughs and the finale is a superb walk along the ridge parallel to the lower outward leg, with more grand views along the coast.

(&) ❶ From the car park on the edge of Craster, take the path signposted to Craster Village which curves right in front of houses to a road. Turn left into the village and at a T-junction in front of The Jolly Fisherman, turn left down to the harbour.

ⓘ The small village of Craster lies huddled around the
harbour. Although once a centre for quarrying, it became
more noted for its fishing, in particular for its smokehouses,
and Craster kippers are still prized throughout the country.
Nowadays it has also become a popular centre for coastal
walks.

🕊 **Turn right along Dunstantburgh Road and where it ends,
go through a gate and keep ahead across low, grassy
cliff tops towards the striking ruins of Dunstantburgh
Castle, passing through several gates. After going through
a kissing gate, the route bears left across the grass but
continue along the clear and obvious path in order to
visit the castle, returning to this point to rejoin the walk.**

ⓘ Dunstantburgh does not rank as one of the grandest or
best-preserved of the many castles of Northumbria but
it certainly has the finest location, dramatically situated
on a rocky headland overlooking the North Sea. Its walls
enclosed a huge area and it was protected on two sides by
the cliffs and sea.

The castle was built in the early fourteenth century
by Thomas Earl of Lancaster. He was executed in 1322
for rebelling against Edward II and it later came into the
possession of John of Gaunt. Although he strengthened it
as a protection against Scottish raids, Dunstantburgh played
little part in the many Scottish wars. As a Lancastrian
stronghold it saw action in the Wars of the Roses and
was heavily damaged during Yorkist attacks. As a result it
subsequently fell into ruin and nowadays little is left. Its
most striking feature is the magnificent gatehouse flanked
by two huge drum towers.

Tel: 01665 576231

🕊 **From the kissing gate, bear left across the grass and keep
along the base of the rocky outcrop on which the castle**

The Harbour at Craster

stands. Past the castle, the path continues along the
flatter coastline of Embleton Bay to another kissing gate.
After going through, head across part of Dunstantburgh
Castle golf course and where the path bears right
towards the beach, keep ahead across grass, soon picking
up another path and continuing by a fence on the left.

Follow the path to reach the end of a lane where
you turn left through a gate, ❷ here leaving the coast
path. Walk along the lane towards the hamlet of Dunstan
Steads and on the edge of the houses, turn left onto
a tarmac track, at a public bridleway sign to Dunstan
Square. The way continues along first a rough track and

The ruins of Dunstantburgh Castle

then a straight concrete track and at a public footpath sign to Craster and Dunstantburgh Castle – just after going through a gate in front of a barn – turn left through a gate. Walk along the right edge of a field, go through another gate and head gently uphill to pass through a gap in the ridge known as The Heughs.

Keep ahead across a plateau to a stile in the field corner. Do not climb it but turn right through a gate ❸ and continue across grass and by gorse bushes, initially keeping parallel to a wire fence on the left but later veering right away from it. Look out for a fence corner where you keep by a wire fence again, climb a stile in the field corner and continue across an area of gorse and other bushes by a low stone wall on the left. Follow the path around a left bend and at a public footpath sign, continue down a tarmac drive to a road by the harbour at Craster. Turn right to return to the car park.